SLATE WRITING

Slate Writing

Invisible Intelligence

Ron Nagy

2010
Galde Press
Lakeville, Minnesota, U.S.A.
www.galdepress.com

Slate Writing
© Copyright 2008 by Ron Nagy

First Edition
Third Printing, 2010

Galde Press
PO Box 460
Lakeville, Minnesota 55044–0460
www.galdepress.com

Contents

Prologue

Old houses have secrets, in closets, in the attic, under floor-boards, especially the second step to the upper floors. Always feel for a loose brick in the chimney my grandfather told me. He contracted to tear down old houses, a "junk man"—so I thought. Actually, he was an explorer of antiquities. He first searched for the forgotten hidden treasures of the past inhab-itants of those houses. Treasures those inhabitants held close to their hearts and trusted to reveal to no one until it was too late to remember. I always thought he was just saving the copper pipes, window glass, mantle trim, brick, and stone to resell to contractors for the upscale mansions that were being built along the main line of Philadelphia. I was the "gopher," go for this and go for that. I was always going for something I couldn't find, and when I returned my grandfather would have this ironical grin on his face. I learned some valuable lessons from my grandfather.

The old house I live in now is no different; there are hiding places…magical areas for a grownup kid like me to venture into. My house was built in 1882. By 1901 the house's main parlor was being advertised for rent as having a séance room, seventeen feet square, with bay window, closet, and upright piano. How many séance's were held here over the years and who were the people who attended on a regular basis? What knowledge was obtained, and was all the information revealed—or was it suppressed, then written down and hidden away? Could I find something that no one else had discovered? Had anyone ever tried?

Introduction

As a Spiritualist researcher and historian I have been asked many times to explain how writing could just appear between two framed five-by-seven-inch slates, placed facing each other and bound together. Within this book I will explain the various ways slate writing was accomplished. Officially, slate writing is called psychography or direct writing.

I was consumed by the precipitated spirit painting phenomena for several years and completed a book on that subject (*Precipitated Spirit Painting*, Galde Press, 2006). While obtaining information on that subject, I noticed news articles and book excerpts on slate writing that also piqued my interest. What information did I find that was different or out of the ordinary from what had already been written? The slates were produced in various ways that for many years were not fully explained, and the professional slate-writing mediums had never been given the fair recognition they deserved.

I discovered some news articles that described slates that were produced by unacceptable methods, and I had the delicate task of explaining those fraudulent methods and the writing they contained. I also had to approach this subject with an open and critical mind. There were just as many fraudulent mediums and psychics as there were fraudulent skeptics.... skeptics who were so intense in their prejudice against a belief in Spiritualism they would stop at nothing to disprove the possibility of spirit communication. Suggestibility or lack of understanding on the part of the recipient had produced imposters who preyed upon the bereaved. The slate-writing medium was pushed to exhaustion to produce phenomena seven days a week and at times did supplement with parlor tricks. The public demanded phenomena, and the results suffered. Scientists with a critical, negative mind set tested mediums expecting foul play; this negativity is transferred into the spirit world and either stops the phenomena or attracts lowly spirits who interfere with or contaminate the process.

Because someone is capable of fraud does not mean they will always deceive. To disprove the general character of the phenomenon when there is evidence that it really can occur, no matter what the state of the medium's nerves or mind may be, does not at all affect the primary question. How does the medium acquire the heretofore-unknown information, and how does some kind of information eventually appear on a slate?

Brilliant minds—to name a few, Sir William F. Barrett, Sir William Crookes, Sir Arthur Conan Doyle, Dr. Richard Hodgson, Professor Camille Flammarian, Professor William James, Sir Oliver Lodge, C. G.Jung, Dr. Charles Richet, Professor Alfred Wallace, and many more—spent years investigating mediums and Spiritualism and arrived at the conclusion that there is evidence for the existence of the spirit after the change called death. The more information I discovered brought up more questions in my mind that needed answers. I felt slate messages were genuine spirit contact, but I needed to prove on paper beyond a doubt what I already personally believed. I had questions that needed answers and my task was cut out for me.

How were the various colors produced, as many as thirty-three on one slate? A white chalk was used; what was that substance and how did it differ from the chalk we have today? Did a miniature spirit or hand appear between the slates and scratch out a message? What kind of people would request messages, and what was their mental condition or state of mind? Could the slates only be produced in darkness or could they be done in the light? Did deceased children ever communicate in spirit and produce messages? I could not remember any slates with signatures or messages from children. Why did two framed slates have to be facing each other, then bound tight? Were any slates ever produced singly, facing upwards where the writing would appear while being observed? How often did the phenomena produced depend on the receptivity of the people watching? Why was it more difficult for the slate phenomena to be produced during times of scientific testing?

I felt I had more questions in my mind than I could find answers for. Should I attempt to write a book on slates? One summer afternoon I met a spry woman in her late eighties. She looked up at me with eyes much younger than her years and said, "I had a slate done by Perry Keeler and it meant so much to me, it got me thru those hard times back then."

I asked her how it was done, how the writing was produced? She said, "I brought my own slates. They were tied with my own ribbon. I put them on the table in Keeler's home on Cottage Row. He sat across from me. It was in the daytime; the room was real bright. He had his hands on the table. Then he and I both placed our hands on those slates. I heard a light scratching sound and he said, 'It's done.' The message was for me, and something personal that no one else would have known about."

I had never heard a first person account of the slate-writing séance and here was the inspiration I needed. This woman's story inspired me to start writing. If all slate writing was assumed to be a fraudulent trick of sorts I was going to find out how it was done and why anyone would deliberately deceive a bereaved person. Why would so many intelligent people vouch for and verify the slate-writing phenomena by signing their names, and send their stories and reports to newspapers, and in return those newspapers print the articles as fact?

One event led to another; synchronicity, the connecting principle. Ideas and inspiration started to flow. A book by C. G. Jung jumped out at me as I was wandering a bookstore. Jung the psychoanalyst had investigated the occult, mediums, and Spiritualism. I had a vision of a room filled with books, then a space containing unusual symbols. I suddenly felt there were principles of the slate-writing phenomena not yet known and waiting to be revealed. Were these symbols some kind of mathematical formula, and how could I put a vision into words and on paper? The extent of my mathematical and scientific knowledge was limited and I knew I would need help. I know matter cannot be destroyed, and that spirit is just a higher form of matter. As fan rotors go from a low speed to a high speed and become invisible, the human soul passes over into a higher, faster vibration where one is still present but cannot be seen.

Experiencing a human, materialistic existence, we assume our outer world of consciousness and time is all there is. If we can unite the outer world with the inner world of consciousness that includes matter, energy, space, and time, what could we accomplish? We will enter that inner world of consciousness.

What is Spiritualism? The space in this book will not allow for a complete historical and psychological explanation of what Spiritualism is or appears to be. Spiritualists believe in the actual intervention of a spiritual world within our world and make a religious practice of communicating with spirits through mediums. Spiritualism is also a science and a philosophy. A science because they record and prove the phenomena by using scientific facts, and a philosophy because it is a differing way of life based on self responsibility; re: the Golden Rule. Spiritual-

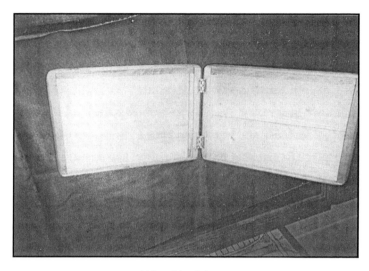

Wood lock box.

ism was incorporated and recognized as an organized religion by the United States government in 1893 through the National Spiritualists Association, now called the National Spiritualist Association of Churches.

Spiritualism as a sect originated in America in the year 1848. Two girls, Kate and Maggie of the Fox Family of Hydesville, near Rochester, New York, were frightened every night by knocking sounds. Gradually communication was established by questions being answered with a definite number of knocks. A knocking alphabet was established, and it was discovered that a Charles B. Rosna had been murdered in the house and buried in the cellar. Investigations later confirmed this and the actual bones and peddler's box were found in a wall that had caved out in 1904. Public appearances and demonstrations by the Fox

Wood lock box with slate.

Sisters of the rapping phenomena quickly spread the movement across the United States and Great Britain and onto the European continent. The courageous action of the Fox Sisters to come forward and make their powers known explains the surprising numbers of others who also came forward and confessed that they had the same abilities. Mediums were heard of in ever increasing numbers. The groundwork was now laid.

Marvelous phenomena took place, quite extraordinary things that went far beyond the limits of credibility. A thinking person who was not an eyewitness could only treat them with skepticism. The impossible happened: human bodies, and parts of human bodies, materialized out of thin air, had an intelligence of their own, and declared themselves to be spirits of the dead. These spirits allowed themselves to be experimented on by leaving behind prints of their hands and feet, allowed themselves to be photographed, and left handwriting on the inner

Pair of slates open.

side of two slates fastened together. Levitation of human beings took place, which was witnessed by the leading scientific and intellectual minds of the day. At least a hundred levitations by D. D. Home are recorded and witnessed by creditable persons. They constitute overwhelming evidence that the incredibly impossible can be possible. To reject the recorded evidence on this subject is to reject all human testimony whatever. No phenomenon has ever been supported by a stronger array of proofs.

Are we today to question eminent scientists and respected people of the days of the beginning of modern Spiritualism as mentally unstable or professionally incompetent, or did they witness and examine something inconceivable as a reality?

The impression received from reading numerous books and news articles is this: There remained a psychological bias based on education, habit of thought, personal convictions, and prejudice, by the scientist and the observer. There was a general disbelief and fear of acknowledging a fourth or a fifth dimension. Allow us now to approach the phenomenon of slate writing from a scientific, psychological, and spiritual point of view.

Pair of slates closed.

What Is Slate Writing and How Is It Done?

Psychography, direct writing, and independent writing are all words to describe the same phenomenon. Slate writing is the more common word to describe writing that appears between slates without the use of a human hand, whereas automatic writing is produced when the spirit controls the part of the brain that directs the arm and hand to produce writing. Slate writing became popular as a means of spirit communication because a message consisting of a vast amount of words could appear without placing a tremendous strain on the medium. Also the message could come through without the medium having to interpret the message or who it was coming from; the message was signed.

The first form of slate writing was produced on two five-by-seven-inch clean school-size slates, placed side by side. A "school slate" was first used during the days of the one-room schoolhouse. Paper was expensive and in short supply, so the children would each hold a small slate on which to write, after which the lesson could easily be erased. Thus no paper would be wasted. A small piece of slate pencil was placed on one side of the slates; the slates were fastened together on top of each other. As the years passed by and the small, school-sized slates became more difficult to find, a similar-sized box was made that could also be securely fastened together. A five-by-seven-inch index card was placed in the enclosed area with a lead pencil tip broken off and placed within the box.

During the second half of the nineteenth century and early twentieth century, pencils cut from solid pieces of soapstone were used by schoolchildren for use in the classroom to write on five-by-seven-inch tablets cut from the harder grades of slate. Slate pencils were available with the slate core unwrapped, wrapped in paper, or encased in wood. Slate pencils were advertised as late as 1914. Wood-cased slate pencils were still sold as late as the early 1930s but were difficult to obtain. The chalk used today (blackboard chalk), which is used on the large schoolroom blackboards, is made from calcium sulfate and is primarily of plant origin.

A mental medium is one who makes contact with a spirit entity and can identify that spirit and give a validating message. A physical medium is one who produces phenomena that can be seen, such as materialization, apports, and slate writing. Physical mediumship done in public is now frowned on or discouraged because of the legal and moral issues that have placed a dark shadow on Spiritualist organizations and mediums in the past. That aspect will be discussed later in this book.

Bound-together slates were inscribed in many ways under various conditions. They were done in the dark or light, held under a table or on top of the table. The mediums at times did not touch the slates and the slates were brought to the session by the observer. Questions could be written on folded slips of paper and placed between the slates; some observers placed the slips of paper with the questions on the floor out of the medium's reach and sight. An answer would later appear on the slates signed by the spirit who was answering the question. This procedure was not always required.

Spirit John Gray was the psychographic control of Fred Evans, who will be discussed later in this book. Evans had a worldwide reputation as a slate writer. Evans asked his spirit control for an explanation of independent writing, as he understood it. He assented, and Evans cleaned both sides of six slates and spread them out on the table. He then asked John Gray how many more slates he wanted. Eight raps were heard, and eight more slates were immediately cleaned of their dust and bunched upon the floor. In about fifteen minutes three raps announced that the message had been written. The fourteen slates were found to be written in full, the communication containing about 1,200 words. This is the longest message ever given by Spirit John Gray at one séance.

Spirit John Gray's explanation of slate writing.

Spirit John Gray's Explanation of Slate Writing, December 24, 1892

Many investigators, who have witnessed the phenomenon of psychography, have repeatedly asked my medium for an explanation as to how the phenomenon is produced. It is for the benefit of these inquirers that I offer the following explanation—that is, as it occurs through this medium: Many believers imagine that the spirit hand is materialized between the slates, grasps the pencil and proceeds to write. Others believe that in every case where the signature of some friend or relative is attached to a message, that the message is written by the spirit personally, and this is generally the cause of much controversy and skepticism. For instance, Mr. B visits the medium perhaps for the first time. He obtains several messages with the names of his spirit friends attached. The wonderful manner in which the message appears takes him by surprise, and he takes the slates with the messages home. Then comes the careful, critical examination of the messages. Perhaps his wife or some friend suggests that the hand-writing is not 'John's' and this fact brings doubts; then in another message they discover that some letter is misused in the spelling of the name, etc., and so it goes. This is because the investigators are ignorant of the laws governing the phenomenon. Now, let me offer a solution to this seeming effect.

In the first place, we cannot expect spirits, who are ignorant of the law governing the transmission of messages by psychography, to be able to send a message until they have been properly instructed to do so. Would it be reasonable to ask some of you mortals, who have never studied the art of telegraphy or typewriting, to immediately send a message by these methods? No, they must be given time to learn, and in the meantime if they wish to send a message it must be done by proxy. So it is in the spirit world. All laws must be studied, and until they have educated themselves, spirits must depend on the aid and tuition of other spirits who have become familiar with this mode of corresponding. So you see, many times I and other spirits are called upon to write messages for spirits who do not understand how, and we may spell their names wrong and make other errors, because we take their names phonetically; besides, the message would appear more stereotyped than if written individually by the spirits who desire the message to be sent. But this is only for a brief period, for all spirits can learn to write for themselves, and when they do so (which they have hundreds of times thru this medium), investigators will receive a fac simile of the hand writing their spirit friends executed on earth, besides a personality in their messages that will satisfy them as to their identity.

Now, the writing is not produced either by personal contact of the medium or his spirit friends. Everything done in the spirit world is done by a natural law, and it would be an unnatural law that would permit a materialized hand to go between the surfaces of slates one-sixteenth of an inch apart and grasp a pencil to write. The principal methods we use to transmit messages are by a law that is beginning to be well known and understood by you mortals on earth, by electricity and magnetism. Psychography is produced exactly as telegraphic messages are produced. Let me explain: Suppose A, in New York, wishes to send a message by telegraphy to B, in San Francisco, is it necessary for him to come to San Francisco to do so? Certainly not, he merely operates on his key in New York, and every letter or sound is reproduced in San Francisco. Suppose I want to send a message by psychography. I write on slate A (see diagram) in the spirit world. The medium being a sensitive, I establish a circuit or current, C, (we need no wires to conduct the current, and in the near future you mortals will learn to dispense with them) to and through the medium D to your mundane slate B, so that every movement made by us on the spirit slate is responded to by the pencil on the mundane slate, and is reproduced. So you see we use the medium for a battery, and your earth plane for a ground, to establish our circuit.

We also have other methods of producing the writing,

etc. One of them is by transference, that is to say that we can prepare sufficient writing or pictures in the spirit world to fill the surface of the medium's slate, and then transfer it instantaneously upon said slate (one example of this kind was produced through this medium in the presence of Professor A.R. Wallace). To produce this manifestation we must first thoroughly sensitize the slate to be operated upon, and disintegrate the pencil into fine powder and precipitate it evenly over the surface of the slate. The transfer is made somewhat similar to photography. The color writing is produced through somewhat the same method, except that the color matter is procured on your earth plane and brought into the room and on the slates the same as the former. The latter methods are much more difficult to produce, and better conditions are required. It is also indispensable to have the medium in a healthy state, free from all the mundane worry and annoyance, with pleasant surroundings, and everything that is possible to make him happy, harmonious, and contented. This is important, and good mediums for this phase should not be overworked, but should be carefully protected by those who value the evidence obtained through their mediumship.

As a parting word to investigators, I would recommend that they approach the medium for investigation in a pleasant, harmonious manner, with their eye's wide open if in doubt, and they will win the medium's sympathy, and thus make conditions which will insure good results instead of in the case with many who, with loud voices, while admitting they have never sat with a medium, proclaim their belief that the manifestation they expect to receive will be fraudulent. I suppose it is human nature for all to rebel at insults and aspersions against their honesty, and especially is it the case when the attack is made by parties who admit that you have never given them cause for these cruel charges. A medium being more sensitive than the ordinary run of mortals, feels these insults more than they, and the result is that the possibility of a satisfactory séance is spoiled by the rebellious state of the medium. Yours in aid to a knowledge of a future life, John Gray.

Who Were the Most Documented Slate Writing Mediums?

Henry Slade

Henry Slade was born at Johnson's Creek, Niagara County, New York, in 1835. He moved to Albion, Michigan, in 1855 at the age of twenty. It was said that Slade possessed strange powers. He could stand five feet from a table and cause it to tip over by the wave of his hand, while a lighted lamp standing upon it never lost its equilibrium. He could hold his hand a few inches from the cottage organ and cause it to rise from the floor.

Slade was the first of the great slate-writing mediums, and possibly the most controversial. At the age of twenty he started a tour of the cities of the United States where he puzzled and astonished everyone by the phenomena he produced. As he grew older his powers grew stronger and his fame reached Europe. In 1865 or 1866 he went to Europe and stayed there for years giving demonstrations in all the large cities and creating a great furor wherever he went. Slade had been invited to demonstrate before the Grand Duke of Russia and on the way visited Britain. A reporter from the *London World* described Slade as highly wrought with a nervous temperament, a dreamy mystical face, regular features, eyes luminous with expression, a rather sad smile, a certain melancholy grace of manner, and a tall, lithe figure.

Henry Slade's usual method of producing slate writing during a séance was to have the observers grasp hands in a circle around the table. He would then pass his hands over the slates. It was said that his hands were so hot at times that cracking sounds would emit from the slates and the slates were pulverized. The people in the circle could feel the pulsating and shuddering of Slade's body going through their hands.

In London at one of Slade's séances he produced his usual slate-writing phenomena along with partial materialization and psychokinesis (moving of objects with the mind). A table was moved and Slade was levitated. William Stainton Moses who had witnessed these phenomena, commented, "I have seen all these phenomena and many others several times, but I never saw them occur rapidly and consecutively in broad daylight." Lord Rayleigh had a professional magician accompany him to a séance, but the magician was unable to offer an explanation as to how Slade might be doing what he did.

At another séance, trouble surfaced for Slade when Prof. Ray Lankester, with the intention of striking a death blow to Spiritualism and this new phenomenon of slate writing, pulled the slate from the medium's hands under the table and found a message already written on it. Slade explained that the spirit had already written the message. Lankester pressed charges against Slade for taking money under false pretenses. Slade was tried at the Bow Street police court, found guilty, and sentenced to three months imprisonment with hard labor. The conviction was quashed, and before a new summons could be issued, Slade fled the country. Sir Arthur Conan Doyle stated that Lankester was entirely without experience in psychic research or he would have known it is impossible to say at what moment writing occurs in séances.

Slade fled to Germany, where he gave successful séances of the keenest interest at The Hague. Slade knew no German, yet messages appeared in German on the slates and were written in characters of the fifteenth century. Samuel Bellachini, court conjurer to the Emperor of Germany, had a week's experience with Slade free of charge, and after a complete investigation made a notarized oath that the phenomena were genuine and not trickery. In 1877 the historic séances began with Professor Zollner, professor of physics and astronomy at the University of Leipzig. Along with Professor Zollner were distinguished mathematicians, physics professors, and philosophers. The results can be found in Zollner's *Transcendental Physics.* All present were perfectly convinced of the reality of the observed facts.

One exceptional occurrence during these experiments was the disappearance of a small table and its subsequent descent from the ceiling in full light, in a private house and under observed conditions, of which the most noticeable is the apparent passivity of Slade.

Slade returned to America in 1885 to appear before the Seybert Commission in Philadelphia, Pennsylvania. The Seybert Commission was a privately funded committee investigating Spiritualism.

Many valuables were given to Slade by the Crowned Heads of Europe, among them a three-carat diamond, which Emperor Napoleon III presented to him. At one time it was reputed that Slade was worth a million dollars. As he grew older his powers weakened, his audience dwindled, and he weakened under the strain and took to strong drink. His fortune was soon squandered and he eked out a miserable existence by doing slate writings for fifty cents a sitting. Slade visited his old home in Lockport, New York, in 1899, nearly penniless and friendless. In 1901 he was robbed of ten thousand dollars worth of diamonds and what little cash he had. One side of his body became paralyzed from the effects of his injuries. In 1905 he wandered back to Michigan, and at Battle Creek he fell ill and was placed in a sanitarium where he died September 8, 1905. He had no living relatives to claim the body. He died in dire poverty.

When it became known his remains were in a pauper's grave, the local Spiritualists collected money to have his remains re-interred at Riverside Cemetery in Albion. Slade's tombstone reads, "Henry Slade, renowned throughout the world as the first Spiritualist medium for the independent slate writing. Retired to spirit life September 8, 1905 after an earthly life of 69 years, 5 months and 22 days. With toil now finished, with soul set free, he now enters eternity."

Francis Ward Monck

The Rev. Francis Ward Monck was a minister of the Baptist Chapel at Earls Barton, England. Monck claimed as a child he had psychic experiences that increased as he grew older. In 1873 Reverend Monck gave up his orthodox religion, became a Spiritualist, and announced himself a medium. One of his materialization séances demonstrated in broad daylight was discovered to be fraudulent. Monck fled to another room, where he escaped through a window. The room was searched and a pair of "stuffed" gloves was found in the room. To give the impression of a partially materialized spirit, he used a piece of white muslin on a wire frame with a thread attached. Monck was taken to trial, found guilty, and sentenced to three months in prison. Later he went on to give many séances that were remarkable and beyond question. They were also done in the light and witnessed by prominent people. Reverend Monck as a materializing medium possessed remarkable power, although the one conviction placed a dark shadow upon him.

As a slate-writing medium, Reverend Monck also had remarkable powers. A letter written to the *Spectator* by Dr. A. R. Wallace, dated October 7, 1877, states:

"Monck at a private house in Richmond cleaned two slates, and after placing a fragment of pencil between them, tied them tightly with a strong cord lengthways and crosswise, in a manner that prevented any movement. I then laid them flat on the table without losing sight of them for an instant. Reverend Monck placed the fingers of both hands on them, while a lady and I sitting opposite placed our hands on the corners of the slates. From this position our hands were never moved till I untied the slates to ascertain the result."

Monck asked Wallace to name a word to be written on the slate. He chose the word "God" and in answer to a request decided that it should be lengthways on the slate and with a capital G. The sound of writing was heard, and when the medium's hands were withdrawn, Dr. Wallace opened the slates and found on the lower one the word he had asked for and in the manner requested. "The essential features of this experiment are that I myself cleaned and tied up the slates; that I kept my hands on them all the time; that they never went out of my sight for a moment; and that I named the word to be written, and the manner of writing it, after they were secured and held by me."

Archdeacon Colley a friend and associate of Reverend Moncks, spoke before the church congress at Weymouth in October 1903 and said: "Monck was a unique medium in several respects. His materialization séances took place in bright daylight. In dark séances things were likely to happen of which he himself was afraid. Often when I was sleeping in the same room with him for the near observation of casual phenomena during the night especially that came through the dark. I on such occasions would hold my hand over his mouth, and he would now and again be startled into wakefulness not unmixed with fear, for he could see the phantoms, which I could not. When I had quietly put out the nightlight he would not sleep in the dark—which made him apprehensive of phenomena, physically powerful to an extraordinary degree." (Monck was afraid of the dark and materialization occurred spontaneously as he slept!)

Could Monck ever be trusted as a medium? He was exposed and convicted once because of a charge of fraud. He had the confederate materials ready so that he could fake it just in case materialization did not occur. Did he ever fake slate writing? Monck was capable of fraud and he would take the easier way when things became difficult; all phenomena should be carefully observed and checked. The physical phenomenon of mediumship is of a biological origin. Spirits appearing while he slept and was totally unaware of what was happening is proof of this. Monck could not produce phenomena at will; his power was something he did not understand. He could not control or direct it. He was just the simple instrument.

Fred Evans

Fred Evans was born in Liverpool, England June 9, 1862. He was subject in early life to strange psychical experiences of which he then had no knowledge. At age thirteen he entered the seafaring life. This period of his life from age thirteen to twenty-one was one of unusual hardship and danger. On his first voyage he was shipwrecked and barely escaped with his life. The sec-

Fred Evans.

ond voyage was one of continual accident and danger. Fred warned the captain of further danger, but his warning went unheeded. The third voyage he was washed overboard in a fearful storm, but with another lurch of the vessel or possibly by the aid of those powers which ever attended him he found himself uninjured.

He seems in his perils by sea to have borne a charmed life. The storm lasted for days. While alone in a dim light in the fore-

Spirit. John Gray
Fred Evans. Psychographic Control

This picture taken by independent spirit power,
between closed slates, in the hands of J. J. Owen, the
time occupied in its production being less than one minute.

Our spirit artist,

castle he had seen a strange man with a knife wound in the chest with the blood still flowing. He reported this to his shipmates and then to the captain and was informed his description fit exactly that of a man who was stabbed and killed on a previous voyage that he could have known nothing about. The voyage continued for eighteen months and was a continual series of accidents. He was informed by his "invisibles" not to sail on this vessel again. The next voyage the ship was wrecked off Cape Horn and all on board were lost.

Evans was an expert swimmer and rescued several people from drowning the following year in the ice-cold water of the English harbors. For two years he was quartermaster on various steamers. Fred Evans ended his nautical career at age twenty-two with ten honorable discharge papers and several personal cards of merit. In 1884 he commenced his investigation of Spiritualism at Washington Hall in San Francisco at one of Mrs. Foye's public test séances.

Evans was assured he had psychic abilities and so he sat alone every evening for about three months. When about to abandon the effort in disgust, he received the gift of independent slate writing, together with that of clairvoyance, clairaudience, and other phases. The following account of Evans' psychical development is told in his own words:

"I first secured a pair of five-by-seven-inch school slates. I appointed my time of sitting from 10:30 to 11:00 each evening for I was certain of being alone and undisturbed at that hour. The next plan was to make my room perfectly dark during my sittings. I might pause here and discuss the question as to why darkness was necessary, but I will not, further than to say that it seems a law of Nature that darkness is necessary in many of her most wonderful operations. The seeds of nearly all-vegetable formations can only grow and mature in the midst of a profound darkness; and then, again, before they can germinate and grow, they must be covered with darkness and mother earth. The embryotic animal is unfolded and developed in the dark, and not until the form is fully perfected does nature permit it to behold the light, which thence forward is its life sustainer. Why it is so none can answer. But that it is so all must admit, and so I found it in developing myself. I sat in my darkened room holding my slates for half hour each evening for two months, and never received a manifestation. I began to get discouraged, and determined that I should sit no longer for development, so I put my slates away and retired. I had been in bed for three minutes when I could see a bright luminous light at the foot of my bed. I thought it might be caused by the light creeping through the blinds and reflecting on the white doorknob, which was opposite the foot of my bed. Although I felt a little nervous I arose and hung my black coat on the doorknob, so that it would not cause any delusion. I covered everything that was white with some black material. I next turned my attention to the only window in the room, and covered it so that not a ray of light could get in; the room was so dark that I could not see an inch before me. I groped my way back to bed, determined that if any light should appear it must surely be spirits.

I had no sooner got into bed than several luminous lights were seen floating at the foot of my bed. Some would be about the size of a dollar and others would be about the size of a man's hand. I was determined to see in reality what they were, and was half out of bed with the intention of going where the lights seemed to be located, when the lights suddenly came within an inch of my face. I jumped into bed and covered my head with the clothes to see if I was being deluded in anyway, when the clothes were suddenly pulled off the bed by invisible hands, forms floated about the room, the whole room seemed to be filled with a white vapor. My bed began to shake, and loud raps sounded at the head and foot of my bed, then on the walls and doors. After standing this for ten minutes I arose and made a light and smoked a cigar. After I finished my cigar I felt more confident, and made up my mind if I heard more raps I would ask some questions. On retiring I again heard raps, and on questioning them learned they wished me to continue my evening sittings, which I did, and from that date the rapid unfoldment of powers were marked. In holding the slates I felt as though I was holding onto a small battery. I then began to hear distinct raps on the slates, and a few nights later I realized that they were manipulating the crumbs of pencil I had placed between the slates, and after I had sat my usual time I found a number of small marks on the slates. Each evening brought new developments, until one evening I found a small letter "A" on the slates, and a few nights later I found the word "patience" written on the slates; and so it went on every day improving, until February 1885, by the advice of my spirit friends, I gave up all other pursuits and devoted myself to the exercise of my mediumship as an independent slate writer.

"I found that each month improved my mediumship, and that one phase developed another, so that with my continued sittings I not only developed independent slate writing but also automatic writing, rapping, clairaudience, clairvoyance, physical manifestations, and materialization, and have demonstrated all the above gifts to thousands in California. I gave my first public séance after sitting three months and a half for development. I found that darkness was only necessary during my sitting for development, and when I commenced to sit for the public, all my slate-writing manifestations were given in broad daylight, with the sun shinning on the slates in the investigator's own hands."

Fred Evans was best remembered for his ability to obtain slate writing in colored chalk, which was not of the medium's providing. He could also precipitate slate writing without the sound of the scratching of the pencil. The main source of Fred Evans' power was two spirit guides, John Gray and Stanley St. Clair. John Gray experienced earth life from 1816 and had a similar seafaring life to that of Fred Evans but drowned in a shipwreck in 1837. He attached himself to Fred Evans the medium because he found him best suited morally, mentally, and physically to carry out the work of enlightening humanity to the reality of spirit return and manifestations through his mediumship. Stanley St. Clair while living on the earth plane was an artist of German decent living in the city of New Orleans before he passed away. St. Clair also "attached" himself to Fred Evans because of his slate-writing mediumship. St Clair would assist in the production of portraits in color of spirits and mortals on slates.

Fred Evans passed to the higher life in 1930.

P. L. O. A. Keeler

P. L. O. A. Keeler was named after his mother's four sister's husbands, Pierre, Louie, Ormand, and Augustus. He was born on July 4, 1855, on Long Island, twenty miles east of New York City. Friends called him Perry. He received his early religious training in the Christian church, became a Sabbath schoolteacher in the Dutch Reformed church at age eighteen, and then entered as a theological student for the Methodist Episcopal ministry. Before he could finish the theological school he had a succession of peculiar experiences. He discovered by providing certain "conditions," singular occult results were at times evolved which were later demonstrated to him as the actions of spirit beings. From that time his public career in the Spiritualist field began. He traveled and became known in all sections of the American continent.

Pierre Keeler had been a slate-writing medium for almost sixty years before his death at age ninety-three on August 8, 1948.

Keeler wrote and published a booklet called *How to Obtain Independent Writing at Home.* Within that booklet he says the rules to be observed in the acquirement of independent writ-

P. L. O. A. Keeler as a young man.

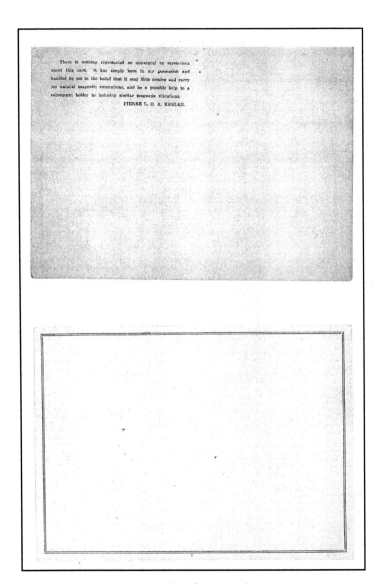

There is nothing represented as unnatural or mysterious about this card. It has simply been in my possession and handled by me in the belief that it may thus receive and carry my natural magnetic emanations, and be a possible help to a subsequent holder in inducing similar magnetic vibrations.

PIERRE L. O. A. KEELER.

Example of 5x7 card.

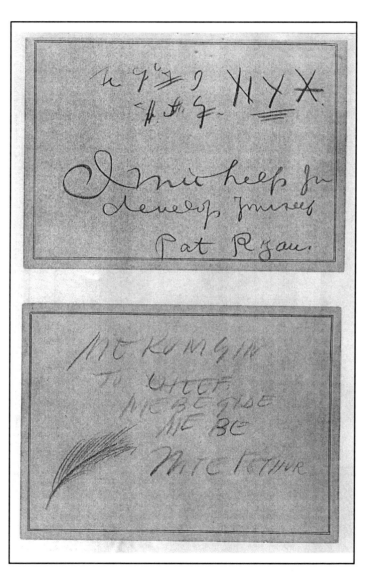

Examples of 5x7 card with writing.

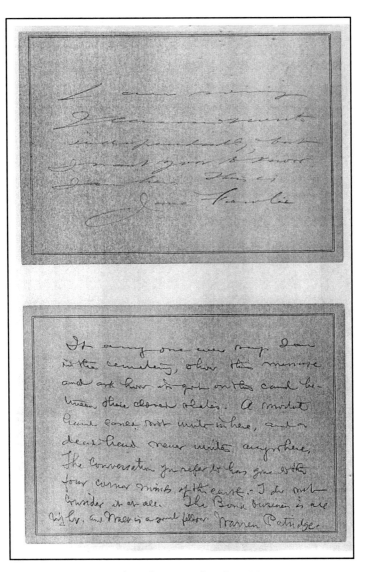

Examples of 5x7 card with writing.

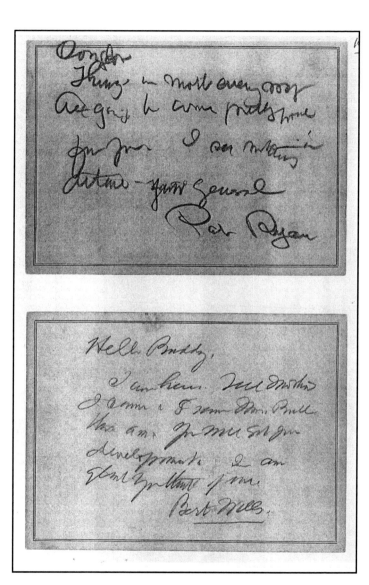

Examples of 5x7 card with writing.

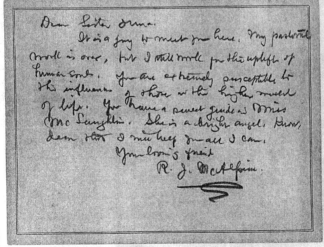

Examples of 5x7 card with writing.

ing are few but important.

There is nothing unnatural about these occult forces we deal with that requires any mysterious, absurd, or unreasonable performance to utilize them. These forces are reached fully in accord with natural laws, and all nature is inflexible and simple when understood. Each psychic person is endowed with a special phase and it is important to contemplate which phase you are best suited for.

If you are inclined toward independent writing this is the way to proceed: It has become difficult to obtain school slates, the public schools have discontinued using them. If you cannot obtain them construct any small receptacles the size of the original school slates, such as wood or pasteboard. Place inside five or six Bristol board cards the size of the inside of the box. Hold in the left hand a few moments a piece of ordinary lead pencil point the size of a grain of wheat, and then drop it in with the cards. Place them on a wooden top table and rest the ends of the fingers lightly upon the receptacle. It is better to place a dark covering over the slates and hands—a requirement which can be dispensed with after your development. Do not be eager for the writing to occur. Direct your mind as much as possible away from any particular person or communication. The moment you invoke, mentally or otherwise, a message from a special person or upon a specified subject, that moment you become positive to the invisibles about you and render yourself unavailable to the operators upon whom you must depend for success. It seriously frustrates their best desires. Sit with as much unconcern as possible and with perfect willingness that anyone shall write upon any subject. Then as one after another of your spirit friends—governed by the several degrees of strength, interest and affection, which they may possess—will gain admission to your surroundings and find you in a negative approachable condition.

It is known that some people reclining in sleep rest better when the head is to the north. The magnetic currents flowing lengthwise through the body conduce to the revitalizing of the system better then when passing crosswise. Some slate writers think it is advisable to face the north and I have no objection. The most important observation to be made in this development is the length of time to be devoted to each sitting. Many persons in their efforts have plunged into the chasm of disappointment and failure because they have grasped too far each time. In plain language they have sat too long at each sitting. Writing can be crippled or destroyed, and the possibility of ever perfecting its development sacrificed by over timing the sittings. Delicate conditions govern our psychic powers and their development. Sit not more than once each day and no less than four times each week, but under no circumstances whatever shall each sitting occupy more than twenty minutes. If you disregard this injunction it is almost certain to prove destructive to your best interests. "Many are called but few are chosen."

Dr. Charles E. Watkins

In the year 1877, Epes Sargent of Boston published an account in the *Spiritualist* of October 12, 1877, of several slate-writing sessions with Watkins and described the medium as withering as if in torture every time the slate writing took place.

> The slate writing was accompanied by powerful nervous excitement on his part. He is twenty-nine years old, and a man of a highly nervous temperament. He is a far different person intellectually from what I had been led to expect. He showed by flashes a high order of mind.

> Dr. Charles E. Watkins a rarely gifted medium, best known in the phase of slate writing, passed from mortal life at Grand Rapids, Michigan, on January 12, 1921. He traveled within the United States demonstrating his mediumship and holding classes. He died impoverished, leaving his wife penniless.

William Eglinton

William Eglinton was born in 1857 at Islington, London, and after a brief period at school entered the printing business as an apprentice. As a boy he was extremely imaginative, dreamy, and sensitive and unlike other great mediums showed no signs of possessing any psychic powers. At age seventeen when his father was having a séance, young Eglinton became disillusioned when nothing seemed to happen and went outside and hung a sign on the door that read "There are lunatics confined here;

they will shortly be let loose. Highly dangerous." His father, not amused, told him to join the circle or leave the house, Eglinton joined the circle. Eglinton went into trance and a table moved. He eventually produced materializations in full moonlight, quit his printing job, and became a full-time medium. His séances occurred in the light and he agreed willingly to any testing. Promient men and good critical witnesses recorded his results.

From the year 1884 Eglinton concentrated his mediumship on slate writing. He sat for three years without any results. His patience prevailed, and slate writing appeared and continued to manifest throughout his mediumship. All his slate-writing séances were held in the light.

Investigations...Why Did Most Investigators Dismiss Slate Writing?

Several committees over the years have investigated the subject of Spiritualism. The two most outstanding were the Dialectical Society 1869-1870 (Great Britain) and the Seybert Commission in 1884 at the University of Pennsylvania, Philadelphia. There were difficulties, insurmountable at times. When a scientist knowledgeable in psychic conditions investigated a medium, that investigator became a part of the experiment and not antagonistic to the mental condition of the medium. A committee fails to understand that they are a part of the experiment and create a negative atmosphere and the spirit forces, which are governed by definite natural laws, are unable to penetrate through that atmosphere. (The Seybert Commission investigated all phases of Spiritualism; the slate writing will only be discussed).

The phenomena of slate writing, in spite of the large place

it assumes in the literature of Spiritualism, may be dismissed by us with a few words, and for a very simple reason. It is so permeated and impregnated with gross fraud of a hundred varied kinds that there is the gravest doubt whether there is or ever was one genuine case. Hereward Carrington says:

> If we were to read carefully through the historical evidence for the phenomena of slate writing, we should find it to consist of one long practically unbroken series of exposes of fraud and trickery, with no real evidence worth mentioning for the genuine manifestations of any supernormal power, nor any indication of any force or agency whatever at work beyond the muscles of the medium.

The Seybert
Commission Report

The great blow to the pretensions of slate-writing mediums was given by the Seybert Commission. Henry Seybert, a Spiritualist, left a large sum of money to the University of Pennsylvania for the express purpose of making an exhaustive scientific investigation of Spiritualism. A committee was accordingly appointed, composed of the following: Dr. William Pepper, Dr. Joseph Leidy, Dr. George A. Koening, Prof. Robert Ellis Thompson, Prof. George S. Fullerton, and Dr. Horace Howard Furness; to whom afterward were added Coleman Sellers, Dr. James W. White, Dr. Calvin B. Knerr, and Dr. S.Weir Mitchell. Of this Commission Dr. Pepper, as Provost of the University, was, ex-officio, Chairman, Dr. Furness, Acting Chairman, and Professor Fullerton, Secretary. The Committee made a perfunctory report, mainly on the medium Henry Slade. All the mediums examined were professionals, little money was expended, and the results published were so incomplete as to be practically valueless. The work was abandoned and Seybert's money abandoned to other uses. Thomas R. Hazard, known as an uncompromising Spiritualist, was appointed by Seybert to ensure the right conditions and the right type of observers for this experimental investigation. Hazard became dissatisfied with some of the members and their methods, but the university ignored his rejection. He stated in the Philadelphia *North American* May 18, 1885:

> I must say that through some strange infatuation, obliquity of judgment, or perversity of intellect, the Trustees of the University have placed on the Commission for the investigation of modern Spiritualism, a majority of its members whose education, habit of thought, and prejudices so singularly disqualify them from making a through and impartial investigation of the subject which the Trustees of the University are obligated by contract and in honor to do, that had the object in view been to belittle and bring discredit, hatred and general contempt the cause that I know the late Henry Seybert held nearest to his heart and loved more than all else in the world beside, the Trustees could scarcely have selected more suitable instruments for the object intended from all the denizens of Philadelphia than are the gentleman who constitute a majority of the Seybert Commission. And this I repeat, not from any causes that affect their moral, social or literary standing in society, but simply because of their prejudices against the cause of Spiritualism.

The Seybert Commission advertised in local newspapers and the leading Spiritualist journals across the continent appealing for independent slate writers to come forward and participate in the testing. All mediums would not come forward. Word had spread that the testing conditions imposed were harsh and antagonistic. A well-known medium in New York City, Mrs. Thayer, stated that the entire commission, one and all, were "old scoundrels and should never darken her doors." She had been sent a message from another medium that the "Seybert men" would do her no good. It had become inevitable that the Spiritualists would band together and their willingness to appear was restricted to a few. Thus the manifestations examined became restricted and the committee came to the conclusion that independent slate writing, whether the agency is spiritual or material, its mode of manifestation almost wholly precluded any satisfactory investigation.

Spiritualists claimed that any attempt to apply the laws of the material world to spiritual manifestations, and the committee being baffled by those laws, the fault lay with the committee, not the mediums. The committee stated that they were continually confronted by the statement that there is only a spiritual solution to the enigma involved in the phenomena. They went on to say that they could not pass judgment on manifestations that they had not observed, and believers in the marvels of Spiritualism had incorrectly and insufficiently reported on those marvels. The committee questioned the mental condition of the casual observer of phenomena, and if the person were excited or deeply moved, the account would be affected and essential details would be distorted. It is difficult enough to give a truthful account of any everyday occurrence, and if you would be an observer of a wonderful event, that account could be distorted tenfold.

Before the committee ended their report they stated that Spiritualists would generally agree that the independent slate-writing phenomenon could be performed by legerdemain. The burden of proof rested with the medium. The committee was not interested in the communication from spirits; they were only interested with the process of how the communication would appear.

The report stated:

> It would be a mere matter of opinion that all independent Slate Writing is fraudulent; what is not a matter of opinion is the conviction, which we have unanimously reached as a Commission, of its non-spiritual character in every instance that has come before us.

The key words in this paragraph are "opinion" and "conviction." The committee as Hazard stated already had an opinion and conviction against any Spiritualist phenomena and was so blinded beforehand, thus creating a hostile environment for the mediums to perform adequately.

Seybert Commission Report Addendum 1888

The Honorable A.B. Richmond (1825–1906) was an attorney in Meadville, Pennsylvania, with a medical degree from Allegheny College. His father John was a direct descendent from the Puritans' *Mayflower*. His grandfather fought in the Revolutionary War. Richmond was noted as one of the leading criminal lawyers of the country and gave much attention to the subject of temperance, on which subject he delivered many lectures to crowded audiences. During the year of 1888, Richmond felt compelled to investigate the claims of Spiritualism. He felt the Seybert Commission would not, or could not, fairly judge Spiritualism, and he traveled to Cassadaga Lake Free Association (now called Lily Dale) and personally tested the mediums. He was especially interested in investigating the slate-writing phenomena. He tested Lizzie Bangs, Will A. Mansfield, and P. L. O. A. Keeler with all giving more than satisfactory results, as the following reports will describe. After the Richmond testing was completed, he wrote a book called *The Seybert Commission Report Addendum 1888.*

My Experience At Lily Dale—Experiment No.1

In the Month of August 1888, I visited Lily Dale, as the Association ground is called. Before leaving home I had purchased a pair of hinged slates, through the frames of which I inserted a "staple bolt." I placed a small fragment of slate pencil between them and passed a padlock through the bolt, thus securely locking them together. At the Association grounds I opened the slates to see if the pencil yet remained between them. I then visited several mediums on four consecutive days, but obtained no results: yet every medium informed me to be patient, and in the end I would receive communications that would surprise and convince me. With the example of your worthy chairman in his patient endeavors to become a medium before me, I determined to preserve, even though, as in this case, I might become a product of the "gooseberry."

On a bright sunny afternoon I visited Mr. Pierre Keeler at his cottage. The room was lighted by two windows, through which the sunlight passed unobstructed. I was seated at one side of a small plain table; Mr. Keeler at the other; the slates, securely locked, were between us, lying on the table. I had prepared five questions at my hotel; these were closely folded up in such a manner that it was impossible for anyone to read them. I took one of them in one hand, placing the others on top of the table. Mr. Keeler placed one

A. B. Richmond.

of his hands on the end of the slates toward himself. He sat for sometime, when he remarked: "My control says that there is no name on the paper in your hand; that he does not know you, and does not know who you want to communicate with."I opened the paper and found it true; there was no name on it. I wrote the proper name, refolded it, and again held it in my hand for some minutes with no result, when Mr. Keeler remarked: "I think you will have to unlock the slates and let me pass my hand over their inner surface." Very unwillingly I took the key from my pocket and was about placing it in the lock, when Mr. Keeler hurriedly wrote on a slate by his side: "Let the lock alone. We will write as it is. Put all the questions on the slates. There is one here that wants to come." I returned the key to my pocket, and picking up the papers laid them on the center of the slates, keeping my left hand on them all the time. Instantly I distinctly heard the pencil write a moment; then it stopped. I unlocked the slates and found a short communication plainly written on the lower one. It was a complete answer to one of the interrogatories I had written, and signed by the well known signature of the one to whom it was addressed.

Gentlemen of the Seybert Commission, there was no fraud, no magic, no deception in this experiment; a power unknown to science had written an intelligent communication on the inside of two slates locked together, under circumstances that absolutely precluded even the suggestion of deception, or the trick of a magician. I have preserved these slates intact for your inspection if you desire to investigate has survived your late wonderful experience.

Experiment No. 2

A lady residing in a city two hundred miles from Lily Dale had written me, sending two interrogatories; one addressed to her mother, who had been dead over two years, and one to a friend who had died recently. I placed the first inter- rogatory in my pocket book, the other in my vest pocket, and visited Will A. Mansfield, another well-known medi- um. I procured two well-cleaned slates, on one of which he placed a small piece of slate pencil. I covered this with the other, and securely bound them together with a strong twine. A common table was between us. This was in day- light, in a well-lighted room. I laid the slates at my left hand, out of reach of the medium. We sat for some time with one interrogatory in my vest pocket, the other in my pocket book. The medium had hold of my right hand across the table. In a few moments he let go of my hand, and, taking up a slate that was leaning against the wall by his side, com- menced to write rapidly thereon. In a moment he handed it to me, and I read on its surface a complete answer to the interrogatory in my vest pocket, which he had not seen. This was signed with the full name of the person to whom it was addressed. The name was an unusual one, the first with two syllables, the second with one, and the third with two. The medium could not possibly have known the name of either the one to whom it was addressed, or the one who propounded the interrogatory. After this answer was received, while we were in conversation, the medium seemed to go into convulsions; he arose to his feet while yet holding my right hand, and in tones of agony shouted: "Oh! Oh!! Oh!!! Hold those slates out at arms length! Hold them out!! Hold them out!!!" I did so, shaking them violently while I thus held them, and in less then fifteen seconds, he said, "There, it is done!" and releasing my hand, sank into a chair as if greatly exhausted. I opened the slates and found written on one of them a lengthy and complete answer to the question in my pocket book, and signed with the full name of the mother of the lady who sent me the interrogatories. It was beautifully written and correctly punctuated. Gentlemen, there was no deceit in this. It was far beyond the commonplace deceptions of itinerating showman. It was a phenomenon worthy of your serious consideration and the exercise of your "trained habits of investigation."

Experiment No. 3

The day after experiment No. 2, August 7, 1888, I procured two clean slates and visited Miss Lizzie Bangs. I prepared an interrogatory and placed it with a fragment of pencil between the slates, tied a string around them, and laid them on a table placed in the center of a well-lighted room, the windows and door being open. The medium was seated opposite me, the slates between us on the table; they were not out of my sight one moment. I placed my hand on one end of the slates, Miss Bangs placing hers on the other end. We sat thus and conversed for some time, I relating to her my experience with Mr. Rowley in Cleveland. Soon I heard a faint noise between the slates. It did not sound like writing, but more like the crawling of an insect imprisoned between them; in a few moments there came three distinct raps. I opened the slates and found two messages written in the Morse alphabet, one of them signed by the one to whom the interrogatory was directed, and who could not in this life read or write telegraphy; the other by a prominent jurist who died a number of years ago. I made an appointment for another séance the next day, and procuring two new clean slates, I passed a screw through each end of the frames. At the appointed time I again visited Miss Lizzie Bangs. I opened the slates and permitted her to place a small piece of pencil between them; then closing them I screwed them securely together. I told the medium I desired that she should not touch the slates, and therefore I placed them under the tablecloth, yet holding them with my hands, firmly clasping their sides. Miss Bangs laid her fingers lightly on the ends of the slates, outside of the cloth. Very soon I heard the pencil write; in a moment it ceased, and the medium picked up a slate of her own and wrote very rapidly the following: "Have partially written a message, will finish it another time. George." I did not open the slates, but took them to my hotel room and locked them in my trunk. The next day I again visited the medium, placed the slates under the tablecloth, holding them as before. Soon I heard a slight "ticking" sound beneath the cloth, and soon it ceased, and Miss Bangs wrote on her slate the following—

"Have done much toward finishing the message, but will have to have one more sitting, the forces not being sufficient to conclude it. Do not open the slates, for we will surely give you that for which you are seeking and desire. Yours, George H.S."

Again I took the slates to my hotel and locked them in my trunk. The next day I visited the medium and placed the slates as before. I waited patiently over half an hour, heard no sound, when Miss Bangs again wrote on her slate: "We cannot write on the slates today, but will another time." I have said that the medium "wrote on her slate," etc. I mean by that, that she placed a slate on her lap, under the table, holding it with one hand, while the other remained on the cloth over the slates on top of the table; and although I watched her arm as closely as you state that you did the thumb of the medium, on page 21 of your admirable report, yet I did not see the least movement. You will observe gentlemen, that I pursued your astute method of investigation, I observed what was going on above the table without regard to the mysterious phenomena transpiring beneath it. In fact, I did not care who wrote beneath the table: I was only determined that there should be no fraud practiced on my slates, which were securely fastened together with screws, as narrated, and held by me alone, on top of the table.

The next day I again visited the medium, and placed the slates as before. We sat nearly an hour. I became impatient; but remembering the terrible ordeal your chairman endured in his effort to become a medium, I imitated his Job like patience, and continued the séance until I became satisfied that no result would be obtained that day, and made another appointment. The next day I visited the medium, placed the slates as before. Each time I had carefully held them with the screw heads upward, and from the "slots" in the heads of the screws I had drawn a pencil mark on the frames, so that if the screws were turned without my knowledge I would observe it with a magnifying-glass, even if I could not see it with the naked eye.

As soon as the medium placed her fingers over the end of the slates, I heard the pencil write most vigorously, and so loudly that it could have been heard across the room. When the writing ceased, I opened the slates and was surprised to find on the lower slate a communication in Latin, and one in telegraphy, while the upper slate was filled with a communication signed Henry Seybert. I will have these slates photographed, and you will doubtless observe the fact that the handwriting is the same as that on the slate observed by me over a year ago through Mr. Keeler, a photograph of which I sent you at this time.

Richmond continues to "address" the Seybert Commission in his *Addendum Report* by saying:

Now, gentlemen, remember that these slates were kept under my surveillance the whole time of the experiments; no hand but mine touched them, not even the medium's; of this I am certain as I am that I was at Lily Dale and conducted the test, and yet the communications were written by an inanimate fragment of stone, placed between two slates under such conditions as absolutely precluded the possibility of fraud, mistake, or deception. How was it done?

Does its explanation come within the scope of your trained habits of investigation? It will not do for you to simply deny it. The fact of the existence of like phenomena all over the civilized world has been proven by hundreds of witnesses as truthful and as competent to testify as to what they have seen, as are the members of your commission. You were appointed to investigate this subject; you are paid for your labor by the munificent bequest of a Christian philanthropist who only desired that you should search for the truth, and when you had found it to honestly proclaim it to the world. Dare you do this?

Slate Writing Exposed
Lyman C. Howe

The Sunflower, April 22, 1905

It is safe to say that all true Spiritualists desire the truth and nothing but the truth.

Strong prejudice may unfit many to properly judge evidence, or weigh their value of facts; but the desire is for truth. No one wants to be deceived. No one desires to be the victim of tricks cunningly devised by conscienceless mediums, or unprincipled pretenders, and no intelligent person will deny that there are tricksters posing as mediums. The most complicated problem arises from the practice of genuine mediums, who substitute fraud when it is easier, or more convenient, than to wait for conditions that must accompany genuine phenomena. Many seekers are

Lyman C. Howe.

careless and gullible, and make deception easy, and these encourage tricky mediums in their tendencies to impose upon the public. If all investigators were honestly critical, accepting nothing that has a shadow of doubt in the conditions and methods, fraudulent mediums would soon disappear.

This would give honest mediums a fair field, and secure the best results. The disposition to accept all as genuine, or reject all as fraud has multiplied skeptics, and created an army of fakes that play fast and slow to suit the demand and gather the harvest of shekels, and demoralize Spiritualism. From conditions thus created we have another growth of pretenders who assume to expose mediumship by telling how the phenomena are produced. They do explain how a certain class of tricks may be performed, ala Robinson, Garrison, etc. But all of those exposures that I have read of—and I read Robinson's book some years ago—are crude bungling and impossible attempts to imitate genuine mediumship.

For instance Garrison describes this as the method that is successfully employed in slate writing; when giving a test sitting take a piece of chalk, or pencil as the case may be, and place it between two slates, which can then be locked, sealed or screwed together as the sitter may desire. Then hold the slates evenly under the table and with a strong magnet trace the name or message that you desire on the underside of the slates. The pole of the magnet against the slate will cause the steel pellet, with it's chalk coating to write inside the slates. Any reader at all familiar with slate-writing mediumship will see at a glance how absurd and bungling such an attempt as this must be. But it answers to some things that are done by pretenders, when the sitter is "dead easy."

Suppose we apply this to such a slate writing as I have had. I furnished the slates and the pencils, they were laid on top of the table in plain view with my hands upon them. My questions were not touched by the medium. As I took them in my hand the medium correctly read the name, and when I took the slates, and held them above the table, the medium took hold of the opposite end. I got 192 words in a fine hand, as accurately written as if by a skilled penman, on ruled paper, and it answered my questions and signed two names, all correct. There was no coated steel to be moved by a magnet, and no chance to use a magnet.

After the sensational expose of the Bangs Sisters writing mediumship by Dr. Krebbs, published by the Psychic Research Society, I went to Chicago from Battle Creek, Mich. So they should have no taint of Chicago morals, or unmorals, about them. They were taken from the pious advent climate, where only Christ and his advent medium dominates the devil and his works. I took these slates to the room where the Dr. professed to have found so much deception, trickery tablets, a trick door, confederate and company and I laid those slates on the table (Dr. Krebbs reports that the medium took his slates from him and preformed many suspicious maneuvers with them) and I kept my hands on them, and when I opened them I found the inside covered with writing in answer to my questions. There was in all the various sittings of that week, nothing that base any resemblance to the methods described by Dr. Krebbs or any of the descriptions of exposes like Garrison, Robinson and their ilk. But all Spiritualists should read and post themselves in all varieties of trickery imitations and in their sittings with mediums, demand conditions that make such frauds impossible.

This will not hurt genuine mediums but will be their protection. If a medium insists on such conditions imitations that is prima facia evidence of conscious deception. mediums owe it to themselves to "avoid all appearances of evil." If they insist upon the same conditions that mountebanks do, they should not complain if they are classed with them and judged accordingly.

William T. Stead.

Prof. Elliott Coues.

Dr. Cesar Lombroso.

Sir William Crookes.

Frederic W. H. Myers.

Prof. Robert Hare.

A. Aksakof.

Alfred Russel Wallace, F.R.S.

Dr. Richard Hodgson.

Prof. William James.

Prof. Oliver Lodge.

C. Flammarion.

Frank Podmore.

Transcendental Physics

Johann Carl Friedrich Zöllner, Professor of Physical Astronomy at the University of Leipzig, died on the morning of April 25, 1882, of a hemorrhage of the brain. He was forty-eight years old, of sound mind and the best of health. Professor Zöllner was an ardent believer in Spiritualism and wrote the book *Transcendental Physics*. He had the moral courage to place in print what he felt in his heart and mind, and then was severely criticized. The *Atlantic Monthly,* September 1881, is one example. Not only was Professor Zöllner ridiculed, the article included William Crookes, F.R.S., the discoverer of the radiometer, and the author of a brilliant paper on radiant matter; William Edward Weber, professor of physics, and one of the first authorities in the subject of electricity and magnetism; Professor Scheibner, of Leipzig, a mathematician; Gustave Theodore Fechner, professor of physics at Leipzig; and Lord Lindsay of astronomical fame. These scientists were converts to Spiritualism because they had tested, seen, and witnessed with their own eyes the marvels of Spiritualism.

Atlantic Monthly, September 1881 (summary)

One opens this work of Zöllner with great interest, with
the expectation of something substantial and more edify-
ing than the dreary accounts of table tipping, and the insane
conversations of great men who, entering into nirvana, have
apparently forgotten all they learned in this world, and have
nothing better to do than to move chamber furniture. We
must relegate this work on Transcendental Physics to the
limbo where we have consigned the physico-physiological
researches of Baron Reichenbach. One rises from its perus-
al with a feeling of sorrow. Is there anything in this book,
which purifies the heart? No. Is there anything, which ele-
vates the mind? No. Does the intellectual faculty grow keen-
er by reading it? No. Why, then, should one spend time
discussing it? Simply because it is calculated to do harm
from the weight of authority of the scientific men who sup-
port the utterances in the book, and because it is an evidence of certain states of mind. Zöllner's investigations
begin with a coloring of scientific reasoning. He discovers
that the habitat of the spirits is the fourth dimension in
space. The scientific gloss is given and it is very thin. There
may be beings that have this ability to work in a fourth
dimension; perchance there are gnomes beneath the crust
of the earth. These suppositions appeal to an audience of
children rather than full-grown men. The rest of the book
is filled with the usual accounts of Spiritualistic manifestations and a jargon of commentary colored with meta-
physics. Why do the claims of Spiritualists all have such a
strange likeness to each other, an unhealthy thinness, and

a nightmare atmosphere born of indigestion? It is not log-
ical to call in the aid of the spirits to account for phenomena, which may be peculiar states of mental action, or the
impression of the nerve centers of one person by those of
another. The first step is to study mental action.

The article goes on to imply that by the power of suggestion, the conviction of one man can persuade many to believe
what their calmer senses tell them is untrue. The study of the
human mind and the peculiar action of the brain should be
analyzed and first understood. When the mind of man is better understood, perhaps we shall perceive that what we call Spiritualism must necessarily exist…

Swiss psychiatrist and pioneer psychoanalyst Carl Gustav
Jung was influenced by literature, symbolism, religion, and the
occult. Speaking in 1897 as an undergraduate at Basel University, Jung discussed the occult in a lecture to the Zofingia Society, a student club. Jung said the soul does exist; it is intelligent
and immortal and not subject to time and space. He declared
the reality of spirits and Spiritualism, on the evidence of messages of dying people, hypnotism, clairvoyance, telekinesis, second sight, and prophetic dreams. Jung gave a lecture at his alma
mater, Basel University, in 1905: "On Spiritualistic Phenomena," a lengthy discourse on Spiritualism in America, England,
and Europe. Jung had a lifelong interest in occult phenomena,
and enough cannot be said to do his life's work proper justice.

Professor Zöllner's life ended before he could further inves-

tigate, research, and complete the final arguments and mathematical formulas needed to convince the skeptics of the reality of the fourth dimension and beyond.

News Clippings

The Banner of Light

Séances with Mr. Eglinton matter through matter illustrated and defined.

In illustration of the remarkable mediumship of Mr. Eglinton, which has awakened so deep an interest in Spiritualism within the charmed circle of the London aristocracy, we reprint from the columns of Light the following account of what took place at séances attended by Mr. J. Mair Rolph. After mentioning incidents of minor importance Mr. Rolph says: 'I wrote on Mr. Eglinton's Bramah lock double slate a question to a cousin of mine, a Mrs. N. I. T. Mr. Eglinton was ignorant of the question. I myself put between the slates a bit of red chalk, locked the case, and taking the key out kept it beside me in full view on the table. We waited sometime, but no answer came, and no sign of writing was heard. Mr. Eglinton once or twice drew the slate about half its length from under the flap, and then slid it back again, as though to cozen the power, but still there was no sign of writing. At last, asking me to release my hold of his left hand, he turned half way on his chair, and taking one of several envelopes lying on the table he gave me his left hand again to hold in my two hands. On my asking why he had put the envelope on the case, he answered, 'Perhaps we shall get a communication.' After waiting sometime longer, during which Mr. Eglinton repeatedly drew the slate out some distance from under the flap and slid it back again, each time discovering the envelope on the outside, in the exact position it was placed at first, he began to breathe very heavily, and convulsive shudders ran through his frame, and at last we heard the writing. After the three final taps Mr. Eglinton withdrew the case from under the flap, and handing it over to me, requested me to unlock it. I did so, and on opening it, inside, between the slates, I found the envelope with (my own son's hand-writing in the red chalk) the words: "Dear Father—W—Y This is matter through matter," as well as my cousin's answer.

This astonished me, I could not in anyway account for it. I took up the case, locked it again, and tried to force the envelope through its interstices, but found that it shut too close to admit the very thinnest envelope. Here could have been no trickery or jugglery. I saw the thumb of Mr. Eglinton's right hand on the table the whole time he held the case beneath it; his whole wrist was also visible; his left hand was held in my two hands; one of my feet was under the flap of the table the whole time. I immediately determined to ask my son to explain the meaning of the words, matter through matter. A clean slate was, under the usual conditions, held by Mr. Eglinton under the flap of the table, I asked the explanation by voice. The writing began almost instantly, and on the slate being withdrawn, after the final taps we read the final answer: "It means that matter is disintegrated by the spirit power which we have at our command, thence it is easy to dissolve ordinary matter, and restore it again by the same process."

At another séance just before its close Mr. Eglinton said, "I should like to try an experiment with you, Mr. Rolph." "I have no objection," I answered, adding, "Had I not better copy that answer first?" "That you can do afterward; we must utilize the power while it lasts." He then asked me to close and lock the case, and put the key in my pocket. Having done so Mr. Eglinton requested me, if I had no objection, to lay my eyeglasses on the outside of the case. At first I demurred, but remembering that I had another pair with me, I placed the closed eyeglasses upon the case. Mr. Eglinton then put the case and glasses under the flap of the table, and as usual, I held his left hand in my two hands. After waiting sometime, Mr. Eglinton breathing heavily became very much agitated; bending far over the table he appeared as though gradually forced out of his chair. He begged me to put my hands further over his left hand and to press it down upon the table, which I did. Mr. Eglinton becoming more and more agitated, I began to feel uncomfortable, but at last he cried out, "press firmer, press firmer; I feel them snatching at it." I pressed down his hands with all my strength, bending over the table till our heads almost touched together. Presently Mr. Eglinton sank back into his chair, and convulsively withdrawing the case from under the flap of the table, handed it to me to unlock. On open-ing the case I found my glasses between the slates inside, but open. I exclaimed "that is also matter through matter, or solid through solid." "Yes"—answered Mr. Eglinton. "And you have, Mr. Rolph, been fortunate in witnessing it, for such manifestations of power are not always obtainable."

The Banner of Light

Mr. Eglinton and His Defense

The value of the testimony to the fact of psychography, given in Mr. Eglinton's defense, (as appearing in London *Light* of Oct. 16) can scarcely be overestimated in its bear-ing on what is, beyond power of peradventure, the most vital and important question brought at this time to the notice of the world, to wit: Do those whom we call dead still exist, and possess the ability to communicate with those who still remain on earth? In itself and its probable influ-ence on public opinion it is a very pointed and emphatic illustration of the truth of various time-honored sayings, such as "good out of evil may be wrought," whom the "gods would destroy they first make mad," etc. for had not Mrs. Sidgwick been led to make her baseless charges, Mr. Eglin-ton would never have been led to place before the world this draft from his vast accumulation of evidence to prove their falsity, and at the same time to indisputably establish an affirmative reply to the question we have alluded to.

On her attack upon Mr. Eglinton's mediumship, Mrs. Sidgwick said: "For myself, I have now no hesitation in attributing the performance to clever conjuring." In reply to this, Mr. Eglinton says: "Apart from the absurdity of the reasoning which inclines her to this opinion. It may not be uninteresting to discuss why, if I am desirous of making an income by my Spiritualistic 'performances' I have not accepted the many offers made me of large salaries from managers of theatres and other places, since, if I am a conjurer, I could proudly claim the title of 'king' of them all? As giving only two instances, a friend of Dr. Herschell recently offered me two thousand pounds per annum if I should go upon his stage (where to deceive I should have greater facilities than in private houses) and give a performance of half an hour nightly; and Mr. Kellar, the professional conjurer, whom I converted in India, offered me, in the presence of Mr. Meugens, the sum of one hundred pounds per night for six months if I could produce upon his stage the same results as he witnessed. It is unnecessary for my purpose to say why I refused these two of my similar offers, but my refusal, at least should prove to Mrs. Sidgwick that I am not desirous of abandoning my poor and uncertain income for a more lucrative one, with the title of 'king of the conjures' thrown into the bargain. And, that I am not exactly prompted by mere motives of pounds is also proved by the fact that the Society for Psychical Research has not failed to accept free séances when I have offered them, or have omitted to avail themselves of twenty or thirty sittings at half my usual fees; in addition to which I have given many of their members and associates large numbers of gratuitous appointments."

Mrs. Sidgwick mainly rests her argument upon her own

unsupported statement that during the slate writing continuous observation of the process is impossible. To show
that this is not in accordance with the fact, Mr. Eglinton
very clearly describes his method of sittings as follows:

"I generally sit in a well-lighted room. My own study,
wherein I hold my séances, has a large window, which occu-
pies more than one-half of the room; that is to say, it is six
feet wide, and reaches to within a few inches of the ceiling.
Three feet from it stands a plain deal table, and the observer or investigator is placed with his back to the window. He
brings with him his own slates and pencil, or he uses mine.
If he employs mine, he is wanting in ordinary observance
if he fails to perceive or satisfy himself that the slates are
clean. He generally writes a question upon the slate unseen
by me, and places it face downwards, with a morsel of
marked pencil on its upper surface. I press it close against
the under side of the table, with my right hand, keeping my
thumb on the table top, the slate projecting about one and
a half inches from the flap and in full sight of the sitter.

"Now, there is nothing to distract the attention of the
investigator, not even the commonplace conversation that
generally ensues between two persons. Frequently I refrain
from talking altogether, unless the sitter happens to be one
who is satisfied of my bona fides. If therefore, under these
simple conditions, the many sane and competent—not to
say scientific –persons, who come to me are unable to judge
whether, with the hand with which I am holding the slate,
I write upon it in answer to the question, then I fear for the
intelligence of the human race. It is not that the sitter expects

me to produce a conjuring trick, the conditions of which he has no knowledge. Here he sits in broad daylight, knee to knee with me, expecting writing to come upon the slate I hold, and consequently he should be able to say at once whether I do or do not produce the writing. The issue is narrowed down to that.

"I am not speaking of complex phenomena, or even of the writing, which occurs, on the table, or between two slates, but of one of the simplest conditions under which I sit. And all I have to say in regard to this point is, if the sitter allows me to write a single word, with his eyes wide open, and with his attention engrossed upon the subject, then Mrs. Sidgwick is right in assuming him to be incompetent. Trick tables, trick slates, and even trick pencils, have fallen into disrepute, for it is now generally conceded that I have the power of going into any drawing-room which I have never before entered, and producing the same results as those that occur in my own room. Thus, in nearly every European country, and in India, Africa and America, I have been able to obtain psychography."

In justifying himself in the course he has taken in thus publishing to the world the real facts in the case, Mr. Eglinton very forcibly and truthfully says: "Were it not for the duty I consider I owe to Spiritualism in my capacity as a medium, I should have passed over my contempt the libelous charge which Mrs. Sidgwick has made against me, leaving my character safe in the hands of my friends and in the overwhelming testimony my mediumship has produced. I am one of the younger family of Spiritualists who

consider that we may turn the other cheek too often; and
I think many will agree with me that the time has arrived
when we can no longer brook the insolence and affronts of
persons of Mrs. Sidgwick's stamp. If we cannot bestir ourselves to defend our common faith, then let us cease, for
once and for all time, to consider ourselves entitled to the
respect of the world; for so long as we with impunity permit these attacks, so must we expect a repetition of them."

Though the London Society for Psychical Research dis-
claims the responsibility of Mrs. Sidgwick's statements and
conclusions, Mr. Eglinton is of the opinion that it is the
chief instigator of the attack; and yet singular as it may
appear, the first testimonials to the legitimacy of his claims
to a remarkable mediumship are from the President and
Vice-President of the Society, from which it would seem its
members are about as diverse in their opinions as are those
of a certain conclave in Philadelphia. As the impression is
held by many, especially by scientists, theologians and certain others, that this Society is engaged in a wonderfully
astute and learned undertaking, and are conducting it with
an eye single to the public good and a desire to gain all they
can of truth, we give Mr. Eglinton's remarks concerning it,
he, as it must be admitted, having better facilities than others outside the Society for learning of its methods and of
what it has thus far accomplished. He says:

"It has now been in existence some years, the primary
object of its foundation being to investigate the facts and
phenomena of Spiritualism. What has it investigated? A few
of the henchmen of the one who is the real head of the Soci-

ety for Psychical Research—Mrs. Sidgwick—have up to date occupied many years of valuable time in hobnobbing (an inelegant but expressive word) over their pet (and in many instances, incomprehensible) theories in explanation of thought-transference; and the amount of verbosity to which the public have been treated has so surfeited them, that the mention of thought-transference is received with derision if not with contempt. In addition to this work, the Society has sent an inexperienced commissioner to India to investigate theosophical wonders. But what has it done in regard to Spiritualism? By permitting insolent persons of the "broomstick" type to investigate on its behalf, has it so inspired the confidence of the many private mediums as to place their gifts at its disposal? Has the Society publicly appointed psychicists [sic] to investigate the pretensions of the many professional mediums whose services have always been available? And why not, since the unanimous body, either pro or con, would have determined the question as regards the genuineness of the powers of professional mediums? Now the doors are closed to them in every channel, and the opportunities for investigation are lost. Is such a Society, then, competent to deal with the question? And has it undertaken the duties for which it was expressly founded?"

Of the testimonials adduced we give a few of the leading points:

Hensleigh Wedgwood, M.A. Vice President S.P.R.—"I chose a book that I was pretty sure none of the party had read, viz., Peter Plymley's *Letters*. I also took a large pair of folding slates of my own, eleven inches by seven and a half, to receive the writing. Eglinton put nibs of three colors within the slates, and having requested the writing intelligence to write in yellow chalk the word to be found at page 24, line 8, word 5, I tied the slates firmly together with a double turn of strong twine. Eglinton then held the slates with the book on them under the flap, all parties holding hands as before…At last James asked if it would help matters if he were to take hold of the slates…Shortly after we all three had hold of the slates we heard writing going on, and, the signal of completion being given, the slates were brought up tightly bound together with my twine, and on opening them we saw the word 'wife' written in yellow, in a large bold hand. This proved to be the word at page 24, line 8, fifth place on the line."

Viscount Folkestone, M.P.—"On the 6th June last year, in full daylight, we had obtained writing in the locked slate, in answer to a question, which you could by no probability have seen, which I wrote myself and which no one in the room had any knowledge of but myself. I locked the slate myself, and it never left my sight from the time I wrote the question in it until the answer was written and read by the company after I had unlocked the same. The answer, I may say, contained a most unusual word, which I had used in the question. The clearest evidence, however, of genuineness occurred afterwards, when Lady Folkestone produced a plain card out of her bag, marked for identification, which she herself put between two slates, with a small piece of lead, which card I am prepared to swear was never touched by you, before or after being placed between the slates, nor were the slates or your hands for one instant out of my sight. On this same card a message was written in lead. This card my wife has now in her possession."

Major General J. W. H. Maclean—"At the close of the séance I wrote the following question on a clean slate: Can my old servant Bawa Mena, communicate with me in Hindustani? I then at Mr. Eglinton's desire, turned the slate with the writing downwards on the table, having placed a small piece of slate pencil under it, and Mr. Eglinton put his hands on it. After a short time we distinctly heard the noise of writing on the slate, and on its termination I raised it up, and found some hieroglyphics written close under my question, with the following sentence written in Hindustani: Humara salam, sahib. I have never been able to discover what these hieroglyphics mean, or to what language they belong, if to any; but the translation of the Hindustani sentence, written in English characters is, I salute you sir. I never took my eyes off the slate whilst this was going on; from the time I wrote the question until I took it up after the answer had been written. I may mention that Bawa Mena was a Mahometan servant of mine for thirty-two years, and died as such short time before I left India."

W. Stainton Moses, M.A.—"A number of Spiritualists met at dinner at Mr. H.Wedgwood's and Mr. Eglinton being of the party, our host suggested that we try an experiment. I picked up from the table a card, on which I requested M. Aksakof to write a number under fifty, Mr. A.P. Sinnett one under twenty-five, and Mr. C.C. Massey one under eight. I

then asked Mr. Wedgwood to go to his library and take any
book and bring it to me, without looking at its title. He did
so, and I placed the card within it. From this time this book
was never out of my sight. A slate was then initialed, and
examined by two others, and myself and found to be perfectly clean. On this I placed the book, containing the card.
I had previously written opposite to the first number, page;
opposite to the second, line; opposite to the third, word;
but without myself reading the figures. It will be seen therefore, that only each respective writer knew his own figure,
that no one in the room knew more of them, and that the
title of the book was unknown to all. The book placed on
the initialed surface of the slate, was pressed by Mr. Eglinton against the surface of the table. Mr. C. C. Massey sat on
his right, next to him Mr. F. W. Percival, then Mr. Morell
Theobald, and finally myself…I was so placed as to keep
the slate under continuous observation. Once the weight
caused Mr. Eglinton to drop it. I picked it up and replaced
it. The slate was withdrawn on two or three occasions, and
on each of these others and I re-examined it before resuming the experiment. Finally came a time when all at the table
were powerfully influenced, as though nerve force were
being given off by us all. I heard no sound of writing, but
I had at a given time, no doubt that the message had been
written. It was so. I withdrew the slate and found on it: The
word is 'faster.' I took the book, which turned out to be Dar-
win's *Movements and Habits of Climbing Plants.* I referred
to the 33rd page, 7th line, and 5th word, these being the
numbers written by Messrs. Aksakof, Sinnett and Massey

on the card, and found that the required word had been correctly given. What opening is there for conjuring here?"

Gerald Massey—"Various other questions, written and thought of, were answered. Then three pieces of slate pencil were laid on the slate, and held under the table, and I was requested to choose which color should be used. I selected blue; and the message was written with the blue pencil…I consider that nothing except the agency of invisible intelligence will account for the phenomena, which occur in the presence of Mr. Eglinton."

Alexander Aksakof—"On the 28th of June, at an evening sitting at Professor Boutlerof's rooms, in St. Petersburg, we were engaged in a lively conversation, when between the curtain there distinctly appeared a hand, whose arm was profusely wrapped in white drapery, and we saw it take the pencil, and heard it writing. It then disappeared, but soon afterward a hand appeared again, not between, but at one of the sides of the curtain. It was naked to the shoulder, and darted to the table, but disappeared, reappearing however, between the curtains and commenced writing again on the table. At another sitting, an ordinary dark séance, on another card of mine, which I placed on the table just before the beginning of the sitting, we found the following words written in Russian with a lead pencil. We distinctly heard the writing being done: 'Dear Sir: We fully sympathize with your desire to prove that the theories of Von Hartmann are ridiculous. He could with the same right speak of the organization of the inhabitants of the moon as of this subject, in…' Here the Russian writing stopped, and the sentence finished in English."

The Countess of Caithness—"I took some of my own letter-paper with me, stamped with my monogram and address, and placed it myself between the slates, asking if there was any spirit present who knew me. On opening the slates we found one word "yes" written in large characters on the paper. I then placed another sheet of paper between the slates, and inquired whether a particular spirit was present and would write. The reply was again written on the paper as follows: "Your Mary will write to you later." I then tried the paper for the third time, asking if they could write a communication on it. The reply was, "Yes, but the slate is very much better." I am able to give you all these exact details having most carefully preserved these papers. We then determined to try the slates without the paper, and I obtained a long and most satisfactory message from one I knew, which I copied on some of my own paper before cleaning the slate for another trial, when a long and very beautiful communication was written in small, delicate handwriting which entirely covered the slate, which took us quite ten minutes to read, and which terminated abruptly in the midst of a sentence for want of room. I then took another slate from the pile, which we held between us before, without placing it on or under the table, and then the sentence was completed from the very word at which it had been left unfinished, notwithstanding the long interruption, and all the conversation in which we had indulged; the second slate was again filled to the very last line, and was signed by the real name of the person for whom I had asked, and which you (Mr. Eglinton) could not possibly have known, besides also containing two very positive tests of identity."

E. J. Lakey—"I have in my possession two slates, one of which is filled with a communication of one hundred and thirty words, written, spelled, and punctuated in faultless style, which was obtained in the presence of Mr. Eglinton, under the following absolutely strict conditions: Both slates were thoroughly cleaned and afterwards carefully examined by my friend and myself. Neither of these slates was out of my sight for an instant, but they were, during the whole of the time, under the closest scrutiny, and this in a perfectly lighted room in full daylight. These two positively clean slates we saw placed together, with a bit of pencil between them, and rested on the shoulder of my friend, who held them in position with her left hand, which Mr. Eglinton held with his right hand while his left was held by my right hand and my left by my friends right hand, thus completing the circle. The slates and the hands of all were in full view during the time of the writing, which was distinctly heard by us, and a sensible jar was felt by my friend when the signal rap on the slate announced that the experiment was finished. We still carefully watched the slates as they were taken from her shoulder and separated, when the communication alluded to was found, and which I still have as legible as ever."

Morell Theobald, F.C.A.—"At the sitting my wife and I were the only persons present with you, and we have for many years observed critically this and other phases of mediumship. It was in full daylight on the afternoon of January 27th, 1885. We took with us six slates of our own, on each of which we obtained writing in reply to questions, placed upon the slates before we entered your rooms, and which were not seen by you before the answers were written. These writings however, absolutely convincing as they were of an outside communication is not what I wish to refer to now—which is this: You took one of your own slates, washed it on each side, after which my wife and I carefully examined it. The slate was then immediately placed upon the top of the table, with a crumb of slate pencil underneath. We then all placed our hands upon the top of the slate. While all six hands were thus in full view, we felt and heard writing rapidly going on. During the process I was affected physically in the manner all such phenomena affect me at home, viz., a drawing sensation in my back and head, and you yourself experienced apparently (and of which I have no doubt) much physical exhaustion. The sound of writing continued for about a minute, when on taking up the slate myself, in the presence of all, 214 words written down the slate in the ordinary way from top to bottom, 11 words written along the side (length ways), 7 on the top (upside down from the first writing); in all 232 words; and one word written and erased as incorrect."

Independent Slate Writing

To the Editor of *The Banner of Light*

As spirit phenomena under test conditions that preclude the idea that they could have been produced by any other agency always seem to interest your readers, I will give you an account of phenomena obtained by me through the mediumship of Mrs. Thayer, yesterday, at her residence, 42 East 20th street, this city.

I called upon Mrs. Thayer by appointment at 4 p.m. on Monday, the 6th, and entered her séance room, situated on the second floor. The room has two large windows fronting the south. It was furnished as a sitting-room, and there was standing in the center of the room a plain pine table about three and a half by two feet in size; about two-thirds of the center portion of each rail side of the frame had been cut away; for the purpose, as she explained of permitting the slates to be held against the under side of the table more easily.

Two new slates about ten by eight inches in size were taken and thoroughly cleaned, and then laying one upon the other, both were bound together by string tied upon them. As we seated ourselves at the above described table, one upon either side, Mrs. Thayer remarked that she feared we would get no writing, as she had tried with several callers earlier in the day and had not succeeded in obtaining any.

At her request I held the slates for a few moments against my forehead, and then she took them and held them against her forehead. Then she placed them under the table and asked me to take hold of them with her, which I did, both of us pressing the slates up against the under side of the table, in which position we held them for about a half hour. I felt no influence, aside from a slight turning of the slates. When the slates were taken from under the table and opened, nothing was found written upon them.

We again tied them up, and wrapping them in paper, Mrs. Thayer requested me to take them home with me, and come back the following day at the same hour, and bring the slates with me. I took the slates home, and the next morning took them to my office, placed them on my desk, at 4 p.m. called upon Mrs. Thayer, having the slates with me.

We again took our seats at the table, opened and examined the slates, and found them free from any writing. Again we tied them up, and Mrs. T. passed them under the table, and asked me to hold them, which I did, and she immediately withdrew her hands, and resting her elbows on the table, placed both her hands to her head.

She said, "I hear the names of Fannie and William." I replied, "Fannie is my daughter's and William is my father's name." A moment later she said, "Put the slates on the floor; no, wrap them up in your overcoat, and then place them under the table." Taking my overcoat from the lounge, where it was laying, I wrapped it around the slates, and laid it under the table. Mrs. T. Then took from a chair near her a tidy, and spread it over the coat, and said, "Now put your foot upon it," and I did so. She then reached both her hands across the table, and taking my hands in hers, she seemed to experience an electric thrill, and exclaimed, "Oh! What a powerful magnetism you have. They are writing now."

We sat thus holding each other's hands for a space of— I should judge—about four minutes, when she said: "If you desire any flowers to be placed between the slates, ask for them"; and I said: "Spirits place whatever pleases you between the slates." She then released her hold of my hands, and said, "Take up the slates." I did so, and when we opened them we found a message upon each, and a sprig of lilies of the valley, a leaf from the same plant, and four violets. These were all fresh, as if just plucked, and had drops of water upon them, as though they had just been sprinkled.

The message was private, but I will give them, in order that your readers may know just what was accomplished. On one side was written this message: "Dear Father—I am happy to speak to you. Bless you for coming to meet me. Many years have passed away since I left the mortal world. I was only a little child; but I am no longer a child, only in tender feeling and sympathy. I have been educated in spirit life, but far different here than I should have been had I remained on earth. The angel world saw that my mission was to be of a greater use on this side of life, but I am happy to return to my dear ones, and give them tender words of cheer of the eternal life beyond the mortal. You have many loving friends here who watch over you.

Dear father, you have many years yet to stay on earth. Do all the good you can. Live true and kind, and you need not fear for the results. Dear father, I love to linger near you. I will ever guard and guide you through life's journey, and when you are done with earth I will meet you in the life that knows no death. Accept this little flower. It will soon fade and die, like all things of earth. Your Loving Daughter, Fannie"

This message, in the character of the writing and style of composition, is identical with the messages my daughter has been giving me for the past six years through the mediumship of Dr. R.W. Flint, of 133 West 36th street, this city, and in this particular message was rather a surprise to me. My daughter passed on the hour of her birth, December 26th, 1865.

On the other slate was the following message: "My Friend—I am glad to meet you, and am happy to find honest and true men like yourself interested in this mighty truth. Tell the whole world that Charles H. Foster still lives. Your friend is here, William E. Kemp. He has suffered much for taking his own life, but he is far advanced at the present time, and will help you much. Charles H. Foster"

You will perceive by this message that the William mentioned by the medium, as being present was not my father, but quite a different person. There is an interesting incident of Spiritualism and Spiritualists connected with this person, which should be related in this connection.

On Sunday evening, the 21st of February 1880, I was present at a public séance given by Charles H. Foster, at which there were present, some twenty or more persons. It was the first time I had ever met Mr. Foster, and there was but one person in the room known to me. When the séance was about half over, Mr. Foster said: "There is a spirit here who says he committed suicide thirty years ago, and he wishes to be recognized. I do not get the name clearly. It sounds like Kampf, and you sir," looking toward myself, who was seated in a far corner of the room, "are the one he wishes to recognize him." I replied: "I know no one by that name, nor do I recall any of my friends that died by suicide, but that is not his name, and it was but twelve years ago." Mr. Foster replied: "Take a seat at the table here and write on this paper a number of names, and among them the name of your friend." While the gentleman was writing, Mr. Foster again turned to me, and said: "You are the man this spirit wants. Please take this seat at the table." I stepped to the table, and as I took the seat, Mr. Foster straightened up in his chair, and looking directly into my eyes said: "The spirit says his name is William E. Kemp, and that he committed suicide thirty-one years ago." To this I replied: "Mr. William E. Kemp was a teacher of mine, and in the spring of 1849 he started for California, and I afterwards learned that he was prostrated with what was called the chagres fever, while on the Isthmus, and that while sick with the fever he killed himself." Mr. Foster replied: "The spirit thanks you for the recognition, and says his progression will date from this hour." I need not say how thankful I felt that I had been able to recognize my friend and teacher, and as I write this some spirit is rapping approval upon my desk.

It is a source of deep gratification to me to be able to bear this public testimony to the mediumship of Mrs. Thayer, who has long been known as the "flower medium," and who now has developed as a medium for independent slate writing, in producing which she does not even furnish a pencil for the use by the spirits. And I feel that I am justified in saying that the conditions, under which this phenomenon is produced in her presents, leave no room in the mind of the sitter for doubt as to its spiritual origin. *John Franklin Clark*...New York, December 8, 1886.

Slate Writing Séance

To the Editor of *The Banner of Light*

While I was in Kansas City lately I had a sitting with the slate-writing medium W. R. Colby, at 1006 Baltimore Ave. I wrote questions on slips of paper addressed to several persons in spirit life; folded and mixed them together, so that I could tell one from another, and then called the medium in. He took his seat at the table opposite me, and requested me to take the slips, one at a time, and place them under my hand on the table. He then placed his hand on mine, and waited for an answer. When his control was ready, his hand was withdrawn and commenced to write the answer on the slate, while he was engaged in looking another direction, and thinking or talking on another subject. He says he does not know what is written during these sittings unless he reads it after its production.

My first question was addressed to a young preacher with whom I was intimately acquainted in mortal life many years ago: "John Parson: What was your occupation at the time you passed to spirit life?" Answer: "I am now preaching salvation by works, not grace or Christ as formerly—John Parson."

So far as I could see, the medium had no possible chance of knowing what was written on the slip of paper under my hand; neither did I know.

The next question was addressed to a cousin; "Ferdinand Conde: How did you pass out of the mortal body?" Answer: "I was shot and scalped—Ferdinand Conde."

This man committed suicide, by placing the end of a gun in his mouth and touching the trigger with the ramrod, blowing away some of his head.

Three messages came from "cousin Fannie," the last of which was written between the slates, as follows: The medium handed me two slates for inspection. They were clean, new slates. He placed them together on the table without any pencil between, and we rested our hands on them for a while. We then held the slates in our hands above the table, and at last the medium released his hands, leaving the slates in my own, saying, "Your message is written." I took the slates apart, and there was written on one of them, in blue and red, a message to me from Fannie. That slate and message I brought away with me.

What surprises me is that the persons addressed could come and communicate on such short notice. I now believe that when we think of our spirit friends they are aware of it, and when we call them they come to us. Is it not worth our while to know for a certainty that in death we do not die? That life is not subject to death? If we can learn beyond a single doubt that our loved ones gone before live and love us, yea more, can return and minister unto us, is not that knowledge worth seeking? *A. H. Nicholas* Bronson, Kansas

Independent Slate Writing

Mr. H. Richards, of New Britain, Connecticut, called at our office not long since, and informed us that it was once his good fortune while in New York City and sometime previous to Dr. Slade's embarkation for Europe, to have a sitting with the famous medium, whereat he received the communication here appended—which were written inside a double slate—under the most convincing circumstances. The slate was placed on top of the table in plain sight, and at about sixteen inches distant from the hands of any person at the table, whereat were seated our informant, a friend of his and the medium. A sound of writing was plainly heard, and when it ceased Dr. Slade himself lifted the slate from the table, opened it and passed it to them. He was closely watched at this, as in all other portions of the process, by his visitors, in a bright light, all things being in plain sight, and deception or mistake (through cleaning of the slates, etc., according to the various hackneyed methods of "explanation" on the part of skeptics) being to our informant's mind an utter impossibility.

The interior of the slates proved to be closely covered with writing, the theme of which was the all important character of charity, and the necessity of its exercise between man and man; the letter bore, as will be seen below, the signature of the Doctor's spirit wife, Alcinda W. Slade:

Dear Friend: You seem to be talking about charity. I love to see a person have charity, for it is one of the fruits of eternal life, and he or she who has it not in their hearts will fail of happiness either here or in the world to come. He or she who loves to do good, will not walk in thorny places; for those that try to do good the divine light from heaven will shine upon them. Oh! Charity, that mighty angel, how few there be that understand its meanings. Religious dogmas are without this angel of charity, for bigotry and fanatic pride are repulsive to her. We would not say we find no charity on earth, for it is not so, a bright star often shoots across the path of humanity in the form of someone who loves to seek out the lonely of earth. And if all could understand how much happiness could be gained by giving out more charity, and be governed by its holy law; more light, more peace would be drawn down upon earth's children. Always remembering these rules, do unto others as you would they should do unto you; walk in this path, and you will always find peace. I am truly your friend, *A. W. Slade*

The writing was done with a rapidity surpassing anything that our informant ever saw. Once during the process, the company—whose members had been arranged after the usual manner at Dr. Slade's séances—raised their hands from the table at the medium's invitation to see if the writing would stop, which it did immediately, commencing again when the hands were replaced.

Our informant's friend was orthodox in belief, and new in all matters of Spiritualistic investigation, therefore he experienced no difficulty in at once acknowledging the utter truthfulness and reliability of what he witnessed, which he described, as in duty bound, to the agency of "the Devil": but Mr. Richards would like any person, dismissing all previous conceptions from the mind, to carefully read the above message, and see if he or she can discover and point out in what particular part his satanic majesty—or, rather, promptings from him—may be supposed to be hidden.

Séance with Henry Slade

On the evening of Thursday, June 25th, a party composed of Miss M.T. Shelhamer, Mrs. Paige, of Cincinnati, Ohio, and a Banner representative, paid a visit to this renowned medium at his rooms, No. 223 Shawmut Avenue, Boston.

Cordially met, and ushered into the Doctor's apartments by his affable agent, Mr. Simmons, the visitors were soon seated at the two-leafed table, with its swinging arms beneath, about which so much has been written on both sides of the Atlantic, but which is identical with the style much in vogue in New England farmhouses years ago, and is admirably adapted for the purpose of giving séances like the Doctor's, since the lightness of the frame at once relieves the investigator's mind from all possibility of conception that machinery or devices of any kind can be concealed about or within it.

The apartment in which the séances was held was in the front of the house, one flight up; the gas burned brightly throughout the evening, with the exception of a few moments, when the experiment with the bell (which will hereafter be mentioned) was tried. The parties were arranged at the table so that the medium faced toward the guests, having before him the two ladies, and on his right hand the Banner representative. The party placed their hands upon the table in such a manner as to make a continuous chain, which ended with the medium, whose left hand was the connecting link with those of the visitors. The manifestations—which were prefaced by some conversation on general topics, in which all present joined—proceeded rapidly as soon as they commenced, and hardly knew cessation until the séance was closed. The following were those which most notably drew to themselves the attention and appreciation of the party: Two separate slates, perfectly clean at the outset—as all present will testify, having examined them before they were used for the phenomenon—were put closely together in the manner of a book slate by the medium who also placed a bit of pencil between the frames; he then, holding them together by one corner, with his right hand, placed them flat side down upon the left shoulder of the Banner representative. At once the peculiar scratching noise with which all who have attended séances for independent slate writing are familiar was heard by the scribe, who inclining his head, was able to catch the vibrations as the pencil moved across the interior surface of the slates; the message evidently grew longer and longer, and presently three taps clearly indicated the end. The slates, which all the time had been in plain view of those present, were carried down from the scribe's shoulder to the table at once—without the slightest delay—by the medium, and being opened, were found to be filled, as to both their interior surfaces, with closely written but legible lines (only one word having been omitted, and that was easily suggested by the context), the whole purporting to be a message from Mary Leahy, of 259 Silver Street, South Boston, or at least she referred inquirers to that place for her identity. She said she passed on January 30th, and that her husband William was the first to meet her in the other life. The writing closed with the truthful sentence: "If people would look more for truth and less for fraud, they would receive more knowledge of this divine truth. The day is coming when spirits will understand the laws of control, and then they will make all believe."

These slates, with their message, are now at *The Banner of Light* bookstore, where they can be seen by those desirous of perusing the message. During the writing just described the Doctor several times tried the experiment of lifting his left hand upward from the combined hands of his guests, and each time the writing ceased abruptly, much as would a telegraphic message were the wire to be suddenly cut while it was in full tide of successful transmission. Upon replacing his hand upon the rest the writing at once re-commenced within the slates.

Other examples of slate writing were given during the evening, the medium holding the slate generally by one corner, and putting the end furthest from himself just beneath the edge of the table—no more—when writing would commence at this distant point to himself, several questions, which Dr. Slade did not see while they were being written by one of the party, being thus intelligently answered by the invisible operators.

During the evening the forces working in this medium's presence gave several playful exhibitions of their power; a chair on the side opposite to him was lifted and let fall to the floor; the slate was taken quickly from his hand, carried across the space under the table and given into the hands of Miss Shelhamer; an accordion, taken by the medium at the side opposite the keyboard, was played upon when held just beneath the edge of the table, the result being an intelligible tune, and not a confusion of sounds; the medium drew a straight line upon a slate, placed upon that line and in the direction thereof (not across it) a tiny bit of slate pencil, and laid a long pencil upon the surface of the same slate. He then put the slate partially under the table, when with a swift motion this same pencil appeared to all as coming downward from the air over their heads and falling smartly upon the table opposite to Miss Shelhamer, whither the unseen operators had been requested to convey it, if it were possible to them. The slate was at once drawn out from beneath the table-edge, when the little "marker" was found intact, not having moved a hair from it's position upon the straight line drawn by the medium at the commencement of the experiment—thus conclusively proving that whatever force which moved the long pencil from under the table and sent it upward into the room, it did not owe it's impetus to any sudden movement of the medium or the slate he held in his hand.

A bell was placed under the table with a string attached to its handle, which was placed in the hand of the Banner scribe. After the light had been lowered a little this bell was subjected to a counter-pulling from some unseen source against that exercised by the newspaperman, which caused it to rise upward from the carpet and ring. This was the only time during the séance in which the lights were reduced.

Mrs. Paige, on taking her seat, had, without the knowledge of the medium, and without mentioning the fact to any of the party present, placed her handkerchief upon the carpet between herself and Miss Shelhamer; and after the séance had been sometime in progress the words, "Look between the two ladies" were written on a slate held by Dr.

Slade under the table-edge. Both ladies hastened to see what was referred to, and found Mrs. Paige's handkerchief tied with one large knot in the center—a demonstration of the presence of her spirit friends which she acknowledged she had received at séances with several other mediums. The test was regarded by herself and the party as of a particularly satisfactory nature.

The séances of Dr. Slade have been so frequently described that further comment seems to be unnecessary. The sitters on this occasion were highly pleased with all they witnessed. Onset Bay, Mass. is the next field of labor for this wonderful medial instrument—his headquarters while there being at the "Robbins Nest" cottage. Visitors and residents at the Onset Camp Ground will do well to improve the opportunity now offered them of investigating the powerful gift of Dr. Slade while he is yet in their midst—an action which they will always remember with satisfaction.

Psychography in New York

To the Editor of *The Banner of Light*

I visited New York City in November last, and had very satisfactory séances with Mrs. Wells, Mrs. Stoddard-Gray, and two with Mrs. L.S. Cadwell; also two sittings for independent slate writing with Mrs. M.B. Thayer, at one of which my son Frank filled the inside of two slates with matter of personal interest and names, all correct, that the medium could not possibly have known aught of. At one of them a dear lady friend, who had been a member of my family for thirteen years, wrote the subjoined message between two bound slates lying on the floor, the medium having one foot and myself another on either corner of the slates, they being at the same time covered with a double piece of flannel and in full light, at 3 p.m. The names mentioned are all members of my family, or were whilst in earth life. I think Mrs. Thayer one of the best mediums. Respectfully yours, *Mrs. Sarah M. Lee,* Moravia, N.Y.

Bless you, my dear friend, for this interview. Your loved ones are all here, but give me this opportunity. I am with you most of the time and try to do all I can for you and yours. You shall be cared for and many loving friends will be brought into your earth life. Many happy days shall dawn for you, and when you sing your happy songs we come to greet you, freighted with love and tender care to bless you. We linger near you in many a day, and here we know you love to think of us. You know and feel that we are not dead. There is no death; the soul can never die. No, my dear friend, not a particle of life was ever lost; not one atom of matter was ever or can be destroyed. All life changes, all matter changes, but never lost; and much could be said on this subject, but not at this time.

Your loving children are here today with love so sweet, divine, singing their happy songs with you, and prayer so true and holy. Then ever be true to this great and mighty truth. Do all the good you can for those that are in darkness and ignorance. The massive walls of old theology must crumble and fall; the superstition of the past must fall away as human mind progresses and expands. Truth is mighty and will ever stand; the false must pass away to rise no more.

We are all here—Frank, Harry and all. Levi and David say tell Joseph they will come to comfort him, and when his earthly work is done will meet him in the life that knows no death. We come to bring you the sweet blossoms of our devotion. Your loving companion and guide... *Mary*

(There was a margin left on both slates without writing, and there lay one lovely carnation pink, two white violets, and one stem of lily of the valley, all fresh and very fragrant—S.M.L.

Golden Gate, December 18, 1886

Independent Slate Writing through the mediumship of Fred Evans, San Francisco

The above [at right] is a fac simile of a slate, slightly reduced in size, written through the mediumship of Mr. Fred Evans, of this city, in the presence of the editor of this journal and his wife. We regard it as the finest instance of psychographic writing yet given to the world. The medium is a young man of twenty-four years, with only a moderate English education. No one who knows him believes him capable of writing such a slate as this; and to suppose that the various writings and languages could have been placed thereon by persons competent to do the same would be to suppose that such educated persons would become parties to a stupendous deception, involving the crime of forgery. The history of this slate is as follows:

In September last the editor of this journal, having in

Twelve-language slate by Fred Evans.

contemplation the publication of a holiday number of the Golden Gate, called upon Mr. Evans, accompanied by his wife, for the purpose of consulting with him, or rather with his psychographic guide, Spirit John Gray, concerning the preparation of a slate, that we could have engraved, which should bear upon its face some intellectual evidence of gen-uineness, as any slate, written in English, no matter how crucial the conditions under which it was prepared, would be positive evidence only to those knowing to the facts.

Our first interview was on Sunday, September 11th, 1886, at 10 o'clock a.m. besides the invisibles, only the three persons above mentioned were present. Sitting at a table, in the full light of day, Mr. Gray instantly signaled his presence by raps on the table, when we explained to him our object, inquiring if it was possible for him to bring together a num-ber of spirits of different earthly nationalities, who could furnish us short messages. He replied that he thought he could do so, answering our questions either by writing inde-pendently, by telegraphic rapping (which his medium has learned to read), or by writing automatically through the medium's hand. He at once entered heartily into our plans.

It was found, as has usually been our experience with sitting with mediums for this phase; that our presence afford-ed a strong assisting battery, and that the writing came with great readiness, three and four slates being written upon simultaneously, and all without the slightest concealment.

The controlling influence requested that we meet the medium at the same hour for a few Sundays, and hold the same slate, when he could more fully determine his ability in the matter. We placed a private mark upon the slate, which we had then held for a few minutes, and it was laid aside until the following Sunday.

On the second Sunday writing came freely upon other slates lying upon the table, and upon some placed on the floor, near where we were sitting, but none upon the slate under our hands. Mr. Gray assured us that he was getting along finely—that he was sure he was able to procure writing in several languages. He recognized the excellent conditions we furnished him, and expressed himself as greatly pleased with the experiment.

On the third Sunday, September 25th, we were promptly on hand, as before. The slate containing our private mark was taken by the medium and first thoroughly rubbed on both sides with a cloth dampened with his saliva—(not a very neat way of cleaning a slate, but Mr. Evans says the writing comes much more readily when the slates are thus prepared.) He then handed the slate to us, and we (Mrs.O. and the writer) were both fully satisfied that there was no writing on the slate. From that moment the slate never left our hands, nor for an instant out of our sight. A small bit of slate pencil was placed upon the table, and we placed the slate over it, with four hands resting thereon. The medium sitting upon the opposite side of the table, touched the outer edge of the slate frame for a few moments, and then removed his hands entirely. In about five minutes loud raps signaled that the writing was finished. We raised the slate and found the under side covered as seen in the engraving.

Two other slates, which had been prepared in like manner and placed upon the floor, with a bit of pencil between, were found at the close at the séance written in full. As the message purports to come from the controlling spirit, and relates to the main work in hand, we give it below:

My Dear Friends, Mr. And Mrs. Owen: I see your object is to create an interest among skeptics of spiritual phenomena and cause them to investigate. I entered in with your feelings, and have succeeded in inducing twelve spirits of different nationality to write a few words in the language they used when on earth. You will, no doubt, find many defects, but we have done the best we can, and you must accept it with the knowledge that these spirits never wrote through the medium before; therefore they are at a disadvantage; and there is also a difficulty in bringing them here to write, for, as you well understand, there is no attraction for them. But I have the medium, yourself and wife, for an attraction. You will see that the languages written embrace Chinese, Japanese, Egyptian, Old Asiatic, Hebrew, German, Italian, French, Spanish, Greek, Norwegian and English. Wishing your dear wife, yourself and the Golden Gate every prosperity, I am your friend and well wisher in spirit, John Gray.

Of the messages given there are some defects, as Mr. Gray says may be expected; but on the whole we regard the writing as quite remarkable, the Asiatic languages especially, of which but few of our own race have ever acquired anything more than an imperfect speaking knowledge. A learned professor, who assisted in the translations, thinks there is not a scholar in this city that can write all the languages given upon this slate. Following are the translations of the writings:

German—I have found an easy way for making known to science the proof of the return of the dead to this earth, and I shall soon give it to the world… Professor Zollner

Italian—I am glad to be able to write you a few lines to aid in proving the truth of a future life…Count Rozzia

French—Monsieur Gray: I have acquitted myself of your commission…M. Fremont

Greek—I come to say this—seek for better things—think well of all…Socrates

Spanish—My Dear Friend, Sr. Don Owen: Rich or wise as a man may be, don't let him be proud. It is from a King, Agesilaus; we have that grand maxim "that one is not great only as far as he is just." Don Juan Alviso

Norwegian—I am here…Herr Holle

Chinese—I write a few words for you…Lu Yeun

Japanese—How do you do…Oyama Gentura

Hebrew—[this is the name of a book describing the killing of animals according to the Jewish rites]

Egyptian and Old Asiatic—[see note below]

My Dear Friend, Mr. Owen: I have succeeded in bringing the above spirit friends together and inducing them to write a few words in their earthly language, as a test of spirit return. This is the best we can do. Good by…John Gray

To set at rest any idea that may be entertained that this writing was a transference from our own minds we will say that with the exception of some little knowledge of French and less of Spanish, the English language is the only language which we are familiar. We positively know that the writing was not done by any mortal hand. As we have in our possession the slate upon which it was written, anyone interested can satisfy himself that the writing is by no chemical preparation, as the fine particles of slate caused by the attrition of the pencil over the surface of the slate can be readily seen.

We have given in the above statement the simple facts; the skeptical reader may explain them as best he may.

Note: Being unable to obtain translations of these languages, [on the upper left hand corner of the slate], we submitted the matter to Spirit John Gray, and received from him, in the same manner as the first writing was obtained, a message in which he says;" I give it to you as received by me. The Egyptian reads: "Yea, the spirit of man lives forever."—Nefo; who was an old Egyptian seer. The Old Asiatic is the Assyrian cuniform characters, which being interpreted reads: "Tom Paine" The alphabet is derived from the following: [Here follow the characters and the key thereto, which we are unable to reproduce in types—Editor G.G.]

Psychic Notes, December 12, 1888 [Brisbane, Australia]

Passing Matter through Matter

In order to give John Gray an opportunity to fulfill his promise to give something interesting for the readers of Psychic Notes, I called upon Mr. Evans again on Wednesday morning, December 12th, for an experimental séance, when the following phenomena occurred: Mr. Evans produced a new cord of close fiber, from which was cut a piece thirty-six and one-quarter inches in length. I held this in

my hands for a few moments whilst Mr. Evans cut a piece
of card in such a manner that one piece, which I kept, would
fit exactly to the other after the experiment was over. I then
held the two ends of the string (upon which there were then
no knots) over the piece of card, while Mr. Evans sealed it
firmly to the card. The string then hung in a loop from the
card—no knots being visible—and the two ends fast to the
card. The string and card were then laid between two slates
and fastened with an India-rubber band, and after being
held in my hands a few minutes was placed upon the floor
two or three feet from the table. The usual signal being given
by raps that the experiment was finished, the slates were
picked up, unfastened, and the string and card immediately examined. The cord was found sealed to the card exactly as when placed between the slates, but on the cord were
four knots that certainly could not have been tied on that
string by mortal hand after it was sealed to the card in the
manner described. The illustration gives an idea of the
appearance of the string after the experiment, and the manner in which it was attached to the card; it also shows the
manner in which the card was cut in two, the two pieces
fitting exactly when placed together after the séance. The
original piece of card with string attached may be seen at
this office.

Slate Writing
An answer to Mr. Coonley's "Straight Talk"

As an offset to Mr. Coonley's audacious challenge that he
will "duplicate the work of any so-called independent slate

writer," etc., let me say that Pierre Keeler has been a slate-writing medium for more than sixteen years, beginning in the city of Washington and spending much of his time here, and I have yet to learn that he was ever detected in any fraud.

Let me tell part of what occurred at me last sitting, April 9, 1894. I prepared four sealed ballots. In one of them I wrote this:

Dr. J.R. Monroe—Can you write a line for the "Iron-clad?" W.H. Burr

I sat half an hour and the ballots were never out of my sight. Mr. Keeler remarked: "Monroe does not like to be called Doctor."

"That is queer," I replied, "for he was a surgeon in the army, and is frequently called "Doc"; and I have always addressed him as Doctor."

"Which of the ballots is addressed to him," inquired Keeler.

I selected the right one; it contained a bit of lead pencil, and I told him so, with an apology for hoping to get an answer in the ballot itself instead of on the slate.

"Put it in your pocket," said he.

I did so. After a while, and before I got any slate writing, he told me to take the ballot out of my pocket, as it was written on with the bit of pencil, and I would find the pencil worn.

"Shall I open it here?" I asked.

"Yes," said he.

I cut it open and found the pencil worn. The answer was plainly written as follows:

Four knots tied on an endless string between two slates.

"I shall be pleased to write something for the Ironclad, but cannot do it on this paper. If you will sit in an evening circle here I will materialize a hand and write a short article for publication, which I trust will prove up to the standard. J.R. Monroe

Then on one of the slates I got a further communication from him, twice as long and under the signature was the word "Doc." But though I attended several light circles thereafter and an effort was made by a materialized visible hand to write a line for the "Ironclad" was not fulfilled.

Yesterday, my wife went for a slate writing. She could get none. I had sent by her a sealed ballot, the contents of which she did not know or suspect. Mr. Keeler told her there was a bit of pencil in it and mentioned a name written within. He said it would be answered. My wife brought it back to me untampered with. I opened, and lo! My question was answered by the controlling spirit, George Christy, whom I addressed.

Dr. Hansman, once a great skeptic, has got hundreds of slates full of spirit writing, and the late W.S. Lincoln, M.C., got nearly a thousand. He would get as many as twenty at one sitting. Washington, D.C. *W.H.*

Slate Writing Séance

On Sunday evening, March 28, 1897, Professor Fred P. Evans gave a demonstration of his powers at Golden Gate Hall, San Francisco that will never be obliterated from the minds of the many present.

After a fine piano solo by Professor C.S. Hoffman, Professor Evans delivered an eloquent address, precluded by the statement that some philosophy was necessary to the digestion of the phenomena. He touched upon the scientific investigations of Spiritualism by Zollner, Varley, Crookes, Wallace, Hare and others of the world's most eminent scientists who were forced to accept the Spiritualistic hypothesis to account for the phenomena. He held that spirit was matter, only more refined, and gave such strong illustrations from nature that it would be difficult for one to remain a materialist under the fire of his logic. As to orthodoxy, he related the account of the psychographic séance with Moses, on Mt. Sinai, and the spirit handwriting on the wall at Belshazzar's feast.

After another piano solo by Professor Hoffman, Professor Evans gave a number of remarkable verbal tests. In one case he followed family history through three generations, beginning in Ireland and spreading to Massachusetts, and to New Zealand and Australia, giving full names of all, with places of birth, marriages and transitions. Finally the last name given was that of a gentleman who became wealthy in the Australian mines, and died leaving a fortune of between 200,000 and 300,000[pounds]. An heir to that fortune was in the audience, unaware of his heirship. The medium then explained the relationship, which was through a marriage of which the heir was not aware. He then gave the full name of the gentleman to whom the message was given, who proved to be no less a personage than the inspector of the Port of San Francisco and Japanese interpreter. Though much astonished, he recognized the facts of family history, so far as he knew them, but much was beyond his knowledge. The medium then informed him that within 60 days he would receive a letter from Australia containing the facts as he had just given them.

While Professor Evans was busy giving tests he was interrupted by the spirit of McCullough, the famous actor who died a maniac. The spirit wanted to control him but he objected. Suddenly the medium exclaimed, "There, he has taken that man," pointing to the gallery. Looking in the direction indicated we beheld a young man standing in a tragic attitude, but in the cataleptic state. Under the complete control of the actor, the young man recited a part of "Virginius" with such tragic effect that a row of erstwhile skeptics, who sat near the writer, and who had heard McCullough in that role, declared that none but he, could act or recite those lines in that manner. Then came the most tragic scene. The spirit was evidently impersonating his last earthly moments. He leaned out over the balcony railing, and with rigid features, wildly staring eyes and the gestures of a madman shrieked, "I'm mad! I'm mad! I'm mad!" Here the young man sank back upon his seat and the control left him with a bewildered look, and in such an exhausted physical condition that he trembled visibly for some time. Upon resuming his normal condition, he turned out to be a plain, modest-looking youth, instead of a raving maniac.

After this exciting event, several slates were produced, and the medium selected John Broder, a well-known music dealer on O'Farrell Street, and Mrs. George Hilderbrandt, of Lombard Street, as a committee to assist. He then wrote a large letter with white chalk upon both sides of every slate. The first two slates were then fastened together with sealing wax, in the hands of Mr. Broder, who then took them down in the audience and held them up where all could see. The lady, who held a single slate, with a large figure 3 on one side and a 4 on the other, laid her slate down on the piano keys, in full view of the audience, as was all other proceedings.

In a few minutes the slate on the piano was found to be covered with messages, some written in red chalk, spread on thick, over the white chalk mark—figure 4. The test precluded the possibility of chemicals having been used. The closed slates were then opened, and were covered in like manner with messages, some being in colored, raised letters over the white chalk letter, written after the slates were washed in full view of the audience.

The many messages were then read and recognized, many names and facts being given which it was utterly impossible for the medium to know. The slates containing these messages are on exhibition in the office of the *Philosophical Journal.*

The Banner of Light, Boston, Saturday, March 9, 1895

It is with pleasure that we are able to present to the readers of The Banner a faithful portrait of Pierre L. O. A. Keeler, whose recent work, demonstrating the truth and power of Spiritualism, in Boston, has met with so much favor.

Mr. Keeler was born on Long Island on July 4, 1855, and is yet under forty years of age. He remained in his home until he was about fifteen years old, when he went to New York City and engaged in the service of the Western Union Telegraph Company. Being possessed of a literary turn of mind, he wrote articles for several newspapers, and at an early age embarked in undertakings in that line, all of which were successes so far as merit and satisfaction to the public were concerned.

He seriously considered at one time being a Methodist Episcopal minister, and for thirteen months studied with that object in view.

In 1880 Mr. Keeler became connected with The Celestial City, a paper devoted to Spiritualism. It was suspended, but in 1889 was restarted, only to enjoy a short existence. There were evidences of Mr. Keeler's ability in the editorial line.

In 1878 Mr. Keeler began to receive spiritual power through a phase in mediumship known as slate writing, and it was in this line that he stepped into instant notoriety. From this he went into light séances, and in these two branches of the work almost exclusively he has been engaged.

Mr. Keeler rates many of his experiences in his great round of travel over this country, going so far as to say that he has been insulted, assaulted, and mobbed in prominent cities and towns because of the unbelief of some of his hearers and observers. Some of these incidents are still fresh in the mind of many readers. With all the controversies and altercations, which Mr. Keeler has met, nothing he claims has been developed showing trickery or deceit on his part or any person connected with him in his Spiritualistic work.

Mr. Keeler has visited many prominent persons, some of whom are no less than Secretary Bayard, Gen. John A. Logan, Bishop John P. Newman and Rev. Byron Sunderland, and has given marked evidence of spirit return.

It is said that Alfred Russel Wallace was led partly to write his charming lecture, "If a Man Die, Shall he Live Again?" on what he saw at a séance given by Mr. Keeler, allusion being made to it in the lecture. Mr. Keeler's control at the present time is George Christie, and the manifestations are true to the earth life of the well-known minstrel.

Mr. Keeler in September 1881 married Miss Isabel L. Leslie, a most estimable lady, and has a son who strongly resembles the mother in looks and temperament.

A recent event occurring in Boston has brought Mr. Keeler into great prominence. He has for the past few months been holding séances in the First Spiritual Temple, Exeter and Newbury streets, Boston, with great success. Thousands have flocked each Sunday morning to witness and hear, and have gone away convinced of the validity of what was given them, whether it were manifestations on the guitar, tambourine, messages or whatever else might come to them. Skeptics have offered everything they could to thwart the efforts, which were put forth, but without avail. Mr. Keeler has certainly cause to feel proud that he has been successfully endorsed.

It has been Mr. Keeler's custom to hold private séances by appointment, and otherwise, during the week, and occasionally on Sunday evening, if any persons have shown a desire to attend. This was but a natural conclusion, owing to his increased popularity and success at the public services in the Temple. At the Sunday evening séances those desiring to do so have compensated him as they felt disposed, some giving a small fee, and many giving nothing. Of late some of the skeptics have discovered that Mr. Keeler was breaking an ordinance of the great, moral, broad minded, benevolent city of Boston by "holding a show without a license" from the said city through its over worked city clerk, and so pressure was brought upon the authorities to chastise Mr. Keeler.

Accordingly, Sunday evening, Feb. 24th an officer of the law visited Mr. Keeler's cozy apartments, which when jammed might possibly hold fifty persons, witnessed the convincing evidence of spirit return, and was so well pleased that, seeing others he felt constrained to add his mite to the freewill offering, and went away, as he says, of the opinion that there was no fraud and no opportunity for any. But Mr. Keeler had taken a dollar or more from an appreciative few, and to vindicate the city ordinance it was necessary to summon him to answer to the charge of breaking the law. He appeared in court Tuesday morning, the 26th, and not being ready for examination had his case continued until March 13th, Mr. M.S. Ayer of the First Spiritual Temple who is his friend, becoming surety for his appearance. What the outcome will be remains to be disclosed. Many ardent Spiritualists have offered to furnish funds necessary to prove that the procedure is in conflict with religious liberty, and will carry the matter to the highest tribunal if required to do so. The matter rests with Mr. Keeler; in the meantime he is taking things coolly at his rooms at 587 Tremont Street, where with his wife and son he is feeling much at home among Bostonians, who are unqualifiedly his friends.

P. L. O. A. Keeler and his guide, George Christy.

The Last of the
Slate Writing Mediums

Psychic Observer, September 10, 1938
Keeler—Slate Writer Fifty Years Service
Many Prominent People Manifest Through His Mediumship

For more than half a century the Spiritualist world has been marveling at the work of P.L.O.A. Keeler, and receiving solace and comfort from his mediumship. He has been a constant visitor at Lily Dale during the summer seasons in that period and in the winter has made his home in Washington, D.C. where he has sat for world famous characters including senators, congressmen, governors, foreign diplomats and others. Marked instances of positive physical results following sessions with him are many. William Henry Crowell of the U.S. Treasury Department in the closing moments of a fatal illness wrote a will so poorly it could not be read and died without affixing his signature. Through a slate writing Mrs. Crowell received a legible transcription of the will properly signed. It was the first case on record of a will being written posthumously.

Liliuokalana, the famous "Queen Lil" of Hawaii, while in Washington presenting claims to this country for territory confiscated in Hawaii personally exhibited to President Grover Cleveland several slate writings she received and reported that the latter examined them closely. She added that her case received much favorable attention as a result.

Mr. Keeler's slate writing has been attacked at times. Thirty years ago it was Hereward Carrington, confidential representative of Professor James H. Hyslop of New York. Soon after this attack the officers of Lily Dale Assembly conducted an investigation of his mediumship.

In the yellowed files of the assembly may be found this printed report dated July 25, 1908. In part it says: "During the afternoon of Thursday, July 23, 1908, Mrs. Humphrey, president; H.W. Richardson, vice president; and George B. Warne, treasurer, selected two from the center of a newly opened bundle of slates at the general store of A.S. Dayton, placed upon the frames and writing surfaces of the inner side a special stamp, whose immediate duplication was an absolute impossibility. The members went together to Mr. Keeler's séance room in his cottage at Lily Dale.

The morning sun was at its brightest and the single window, as well as door, stood wide open. Each visitor wrote her, or his, own name upon a separate slip of paper, folded it tightly and deposited it upon the table beside the slates. No names of friends in spirit life were at any time written by the sitters.

Slate signatures.

"Neither the slips, the slates, or Mr. Keeler's hands were for one instant out of sight of three pair of watchful eyes." During the sitting words written in green color, appeared upon the paper bearing Dr. Warne's signature. The paper at no time had been unfolded. The message read: "It is difficult to get anything on slates not magnetized."

"At the close of the sitting lasting one and one-quarter hours, there were found upon the inside of the slates, one message from a brother of Mr. Richardson; four messages for Mrs. Humphrey and her immediate family; two messages for Dr. Warne; and one for an unidentified personality. One was written in yellow, but the others in common slate pencil, a small point which was placed between the slates at the beginning of the séance."

Conclusion of Investigators

The investigators concluded "The messages were not written in advance—a substitution of slates was impossible—Mr. Keeler could not have written them during the sitting, for he could not have gained access to the inside surfaces where they were found without immediate detection."

Another section of the board conducted another investigation the following day taking similar precautions and received eleven messages in all, one in Greek, one in German, one in French, one in Swedish and one in Japanese or Chinese. Linguists available at the time pronounced the Greek, French and Swedish messages grammatically correct. The report is signed by all six members of the board who took part in the investigation.

Message from Lincoln

Mr. Keeler in his slate writings has brought many messages from prominent people in the spirit life. Many times Abraham Lincoln indicated his presence by signing his name. Many claim Lincoln was a Spiritualist or at least believed in its powers and has sent messages through the mediumship of Mr. Keeler.

W.H. Plummer once recorded in a pamphlet describing one of the séances at which President Lincoln received advice through the mediumship of Nettie Colburn, later Mrs. Maynard, the confirmation in a slate message from Lincoln important facts brought out in the Colburn séance.

Miss Colburn in trance had spoken in a manner that reminded those present of the great Daniel Webster. Mr. Plummer's message was from Webster himself who said that it was in reality he who urged the promulgation of the Emancipation Proclamation through the mediumship of Miss Colburn. Following the Webster message came one from Lincoln himself who said that he had since learned that Webster inspired the Proclamation.

Down through the years Mr. Keeler has continued to give important messages to both the great and the lowly that have influenced thousands in countless ways. Still he holds forth in his modest cottage in Lily Dale and at his home in Washington, the veteran of all the mediums and the greatest of all slate writers.

The Psychic Observer, September 10, 1943

Remarkable Slate Writing

Through the Mediumship of P. L. O. A. Keeler

(Taken from *The Sunflower,* July 20, 1912)

On Monday morning, following the close of the assembly at Lily Dale, N.Y. in 1911, the writer Frank Walker, editor of *The Sunflower,* went to the cottage of Pierre L. O. A. Keeler to try for an independent slate writing. The slates used for the experiment were not those, of which Mr. Keeler kept a supply on hand, but new and larger ones, secured elsewhere by me.

The principal object in taking my own slates was that I wanted it a complete test case, to meet the cavil of critics, if any there were, should I succeed in getting writing, and also to thoroughly satisfy myself as to whether or not there was any trickery, as I had never had a sitting with Mr. Keeler before.

There is no reason on my part to suppose that the quantity of slates Mr. Keeler keeps on hand has been tampered with, for they are new slates, with the original velvet or dusty appearance that new slates always have, and one can have his pick of them, but I took my own.

Room Well Lighted

Before going to the Keeler cottage, at my lodging place I wrote the names of several friends who are in spirit life, on slips of paper, folding them tightly several times, having understood that the medium usually required them.

SPIRITUALISM'S PICTORIAL JOURNAL

TRUTH

ᴇ PSYCHIC *Observer*

S, Inc., Lily Dale, N. Y., U. S. A.   SEMI-MONTHLY   SEPT. 10th, 1943   10 CENTS

EXACT REPRODUCTION OF SLATE AND EXTRAORDINARY WRITING

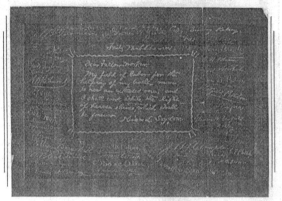

Above is a reproduction of the slate-writing received by Frank WALKER at LILY DALE, N. Y. in 1911   Note Frank Walker's signature on the wood border of the slate, lower right center; also by turning the picture upside down another Walker signature is faintly discernable on the wood frame to the right. This signature "Frank Walker" was written on the slates, for test purposes, before they were taken to Keeler, thus preventing what is termed as "switching slates."

Starting at the upper left, and then clock-wise, the names read as follows: Wm. W. L. BAKER; A. B. GUNNISON; Carolina HENDERSON; Chas. A. WHITEY; S. J. SKIDMORE, after whom the Lily Dale library was named; Sam McGEE; Gen. W. TAYLOR; Lydia DECKER; A. D. RICHMOND; R. S. LILLIE; Harrison D. BARRETT, first President of The National Spiritualist Association; I. Frank BAXTER; Euclid TRAIN; Cass CARROLL; Freeman S. JONES; Elisha Kent KANE; Lizzie E. W. SMITH; William BARNSDALL; Amelia Colby LUTHER; A. B. CALDWELL, father of Esther C. Humphrey; Belle JOSLYN; Daniel A. BAILEY; Susan B. ANTHONY, noted woman suffrage leader; Jos. McCLELLAN; Catherine A. BOWERS; HIRAM CORSON, who during his life-time translated Keeler's foreign language slate-writings; Isaac ALLEN; Amanda WALKER; Margaret Fox KANE, one of the "Fox Sisters"; Reuben CARROLL, Lizzie SHER- MAN; J. B. F. CHAMPLIN, Addison O. READ; Eliza COOK; Isaac LONG; A. B. SWAN; C. T. PHILLIPS; Martha F. FULLER; Bernie RAMSDELL; Harry HOLLY; Nellie WARREN; Glenn W. SCOFIELD; Betsey SULLY; John PROP- ER; Hatfield PETTIBONE, who during his life-time was a famous partial materialization medium; Mary Jane CRILLY; James D. PALMER; Fred NICOLS, old-time Lily Dale band-leader; N. W. OSTROM; Harry BRADLEY; E. C. HUB- BARD; Lib BADGER; Sidney KELSEY; C. W. SCOFIELD; "IKEY," known as "Uncle Ike," spirit collaborator of Flo Cornell, noted "rapping medium"; Fritz MUHLHAUSER; Nettie MUHLHAUSER; Grover W. GASTON; Levi EDDY; and Luther COLBY, former editor of the "Banner of Light."

Fifty-six signatures surround the oblong in the center, in which the message to Mr. Walker (Dear Co-Worker) is writ- ten. This message, signed by Hiram L. Suydam, was written in gold.

Slate with names.

On the way to the Keeler cottage it occurred to me that I had not thought of or requested communications from three old friends and prominent speakers who had passed over in recent years. I sat on a park seat and as I was writing their names I remembered that one of them had objected to speaking at some meeting where the other was to speak, and so I hesitated, then, mentally, hoped if their names appeared that both would not be on the same slate. Their names were written and they were on different slates.

On arrival at Keeler's we repaired to the room used for sittings. It was well lighted by daylight and there were no shadowy places. The tables at which we were to sit I thoroughly examined all over. It is a common, flat top, wooden table, with no secret compartments or wire connections, and is quite wide, so that it would have been impossible for Mr. Keeler to reach across it without it being known. He sat on one side, I on the other.

The four slates I placed on the table at my right, not near him. He sat in his chair, naturally, away from the table. I observed him closely all the time. He could in no way have changed the slates with mine, and at all times his hands were in my sight. A small box on the table I examined, but it was nothing but a receptacle with a cover and in no way had any connection with what transpired.

All in Clear Sight

After sitting a few minutes, I making some inquires, at all times keeping strict watch of every movement of Mr. Keeler, he said to place two slates on the table. I did so, putting my hands upon them, following which he placed both his hands on them. Quickly after holding the slates above the table, my fingers on Keeler's, no motion or vibration made by his hands, fingers or thumbs, all in clear sight, a noise was heard like that produced in writing on a slate with slate pencil.

Within five minutes he let go of the slates. I opened them and on one there were seven communications, three like slate pencil writing, and the bit of pencil that was rough at each end when put in, was worn smooth, showing that it had been used. There were, also, writings in red, in green and in black.

Lyman C. Howe

Two writings nearly filled the slate, the longest being signed by my mother's name, which, with the writing above, was all a facsimile of her writing when she was here in earth life, from which she departed in 1890. The other was from Lyman C. Howe. Both were expressive, well written and punctuated and had applicable meaning to myself, with references to others by name to whom only the meaning could apply.

At each side was a single line, written one letter under the other, one signed by my grandmother's name, the other by a brother who passed away before I was born, neither of whom I had thought of, or that the medium knew of. Diagonally across the two long communications was a short and very expressive sentence, signed with my father's name, in black. At the extreme ends of the slate, on one was a brief message in red, signed Carrie E. S. Twing, and at the other end, one in green, which said, "Bro. Walker, I haven't found my namesake yet. Moses Hull."

Gold Writing

The last slates, after the bit of pencil was put in, were grasped firmly, Mr. Keeler taking hold after me, my hands touching his. I asked if he thought we could get any writing in gold, having learned that he had recently received such writing, it having, it was alleged, come to him through the power of the spirit known as Uncle Ike, who is the controlling force in the spirit rappings obtained by Miss Floy Cottrell.

He said he could not tell, but put gold on the slate. I laid a watch fob on top of the slate, keeping hold of slates with the other hand. Presently the slates began to shake and a loud scratching noise was heard, followed by rapid, light sounds, as of the pencil. Keeler said whenever the gilt or gold writing occurred the loud noise was noticed.

While this was occurring we held the slates six inches or more above the table. Both hands of each grasping firmly, my fingers covering each of the fingers underneath. None of the fingers moved at any time, so that he could not have produced the noises by scratching the underside of the slate with fingernails. Within five minutes he let go and I opened the slates and was utterly astonished to see one slate literally filled with names, except in the center.

The picture herewith is an engraving made from photographs and tracings photographed of the slate last mentioned, and contains sixty names written by slate pencil,

and the panel or frame in center and message and signature are golden on the slate, apparently like a gold paint put
over a sizing.

Susan B. Anthony

Most of the names are facsimiles of the signatures of the
persons when in this life, but few were persons I had in
mind at any time connecting with this séance, a number I
was never acquainted with, personally, and a few were
unknown to me, though some of those have since been recognized by persons who have seen the slate. Mr. Keeler said
he had never had so many names appear on one slate before.
A number of the names are of people that Mr. Keeler never
knew, friends and relatives; others are old workers in Spiritualism and residents of Lily Dale.

Hiram Corson, whose peculiar signature is seen, was
recognized by a Cornellian friend, who said he had seen
much of the writing, and that it was always in that style. He
was professor of languages at Cornell some years ago. Susan
B. Anthony, and other names, will be easily recognized by
those familiar with their writing.

Picture Exact Size

Showing the slates to the daughter of the E. C. Hubbard
whose name appears at upper right corner, she said it was
as perfect a specimen of his writing as could be, that he
always made the b's with hardly any loop above.

There is much else that could be said, but the story is

now long. The picture is exact size of slate. It required several exposures in photography to make the engraving. The slate frame is a half tone, the slate zinc etching and the gold had to first be traced by the photographer before a negative that was sharp enough could be had. My name on frame which shows heaviest I traced on with a pencil, to be sure of its showing up plain in engraving.

This I know, that the séance in no way corresponded to the one described as having occurred when Hereward Carrington pretended to make an expose of Keeler's methods. There was no trickery. I was not hypnotized.

I know, absolutely, that I did not write the names or messages on the slates. I know absolutely, that Mr. Keeler did not write them. I also know that no writing or marks of any nature were on the slates before closing them. All that appears in the picture is a reproduction of what came on the slate within five minutes time. The names speak for them selves, for in many cases they are like the writing of the originals of the names wrote when inhabiting earth forms.

At no time were the slips of paper I had written names on were referred to, used or touched by Mr. Keeler or myself after I had laid them on the table, and only part of those names appeared on either slate, but nearly all the names that did appear I had not thought of, at all, and a number neither Mr. Keeler or myself knew.

The photographers and engravers, who are experts, found difficulty in reproducing. The above statement is true.

Leonora Piper.

Dr. J. M. Peebles.

Luther Colby.

H. D. Barrett.

Carrie Swenson.

Eusapia Paladino

Frank Carpenter.

Mrs. L. A. S. Nourse.

Dr. J. V. Mansfield.

Andrew Jackson Davis.

Lizzie and May Bangs.

Dr. Joseph Beals.

Mrs. Reynolds.

Mrs. C. D. Pruden.

Mrs. A. E. Sheets.

Nellie S. Baade.

Giles B. Stebbins.

Daniel Dunglas Home.

W. Stainton Moses.

Dr. W. A. Mansfield.

Emma Hardinge Britten.

Slate writing given through the mediumship of Fred Evans
at a select séance of personal friends of J. J. Owen.

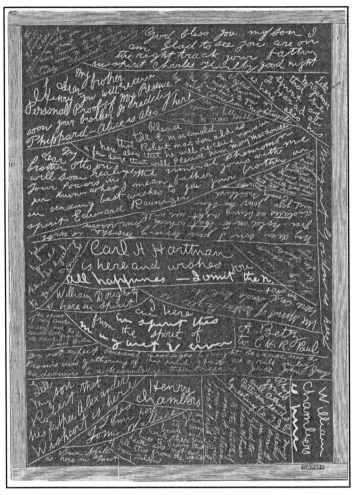

Facsimile of psychographic writing produced on a
slate before the Brisbane Psychological Society,
October 24, 1888, through the mediumship of Fred Evans.

Drawing of Robert Hare obtained through
the mediumship of Fred Evans at a public
séance given in San Jose, California, April 2, 1887.

Spirit Josephine

St Clair!

The likeness, as she appears in spirit life, of a beautiful young sister of Mrs. Mattie P. Owen. The picture, of which the above is a copy, was taken through the mediumship of Fred Evans, in the presence of J. J. Owen, upon the under surface of a single slate placed upon a table in full light and under Mrs. Owen's hands. Time, about five minutes.

Drawing of John Pierpoint taken independently, between closed slates,through the mediumship of Fred Evans, at a private séance given to Prof. Alred R. Wallace, May 27, 1887.

Spirit Camelia. Taken independently
through the mediumship of Fred Evans.

Example of a Fred Evans slate
production that has been traced over with ink.

Conclusion

I started writing this book with several intentions, some of which changed in the process. Originally I was trying to find a common moral or psychological connection with the type of person who was the professional slate-writing medium. I found no connection. None of the pioneer slate-writing mediums died wealthy, none were insane, and all but one were virtually forgotten past the early twentieth century.

I found only one instance of possible fraud contained within the news articles. Mrs. Thayer of Boston had asked Mr. Clark during the séance to wrap the slates in his overcoat, which he had to get in an adjacent room. This was a definite distraction and one among several others during the séance. It seemed Mrs. Thayer was struggling at the time with enough energy or magnetism and could have resorted to alternative methods to produce satisfactory results. Did the end result justify the means? Mr. Clark was completely satisfied with the message written on the slates and the flowers that appeared. Mr. Clark was also naïve. He had been to another medium within the same city of

Boston for the past six years. Were those mediums in collusion with each other? The question presents itself again. If someone is capable of fraud, will they always resort to it?

What I did find were mediums, both men and women, who had extraordinary powers beyond what science could explain with the knowledge available in those days. Sincere investigators, scientists, psychologists, educators, media representatives, and lay people, one and all were trying their best to understand this new phenomenon that was sweeping across the civilized world.

Most news articles described the slate-writing séance in explicit detail for the sole reason that slate writers were under constant observation for questionable procedures such as a darkened room, a piece of chalk stuck between the fingernail and meat of the thumb, or a slate pre-written on and then switched during the séance. It had been repeatedly noted that the slates were "clean," this mentioned because another fraudulent method of producing slate writing was to pre-write a message, then cover the slate over with a film of powder or an oily substance. That substance could be secretly cleaned off while the slates were concealed and thus a confederate message would be revealed after the séance. The people who wrote the news articles wanted to make it perfectly clear that they were not fooled or hoodwinked. There were many ways a magician could try to duplicate a slate-writing séance. As this book has verified, all slate writing could not be duplicated or explained by the best magician's or investigators of the day. Why? Evidently there was some out of the ordinary technology and spirit forces doing some very wonderful things.

I also discovered why some slates that can still be displayed today appear to be "questionable." The photographer, attempting to have the slate writing appear darker on the negative plate for reproduction in the newspaper article, carefully traced over the original slate writing in ink. That at the time seemed the best way to present to the readers the phenomena of slate writing, but has bewildered investigators for decades and has ruined the chances of further investigation on some slates.

It was a battle with cold-blooded materialism vs. Spiritualism. Doubts are stubborn things, and whoever investigated the phenomenon of slate writing started out with doubts that were difficult to overcome. Science during the middle of the 1800s to the beginning of the twentieth century and even to this day is discovering and inventing incredible mind-boggling contraptions that most people do not understand but accept in their everyday lives. Science has gained an infallibility that is accepted almost unquestionably, regardless of one's understanding.

If there is or could be a mathematical formula to establish beyond a doubt that once one leaves this earth plane, spirit can still physically communicate, that would be a major breakthrough in proving the slate-writing phenomena. Each medium has a different vibration, and that would place another unknown factor within the formula.

We know that mentally the spirit can eventually communicate; that phenomenon has been proven by the mediums. Can we mortals imagine what a shock the change we call death is to the deceased? How difficult is it for the spirit to get accustomed to the new environment and communicate those scenes and feelings from the spirit world? Earth memories for the spirit can fade as fast as our dreams upon waking in the morning, and confused communications can occur. A new spirit is perhaps also limited in its explanation of the unexplainable. While on earth, as an example; to explain what an orange looks like one would start by saying it is yellowish orange in color, round, has a certain approximate weight and an uneven texture. But if that orange has no color, absolutely no color, it would be invisible. How then would you explain what that orange looked like? You could feel it, touch it, and know you had something in your hand, but what? How would you explain to someone who had never seen an orange what it was?

In due respect, the majority of messages that were appearing on the slates were kept simple and uncomplicated. That was apparently the easiest way or the only way in that era in which spirit was capable of communicating. Our world is a world of senses: we see, hear, feel, smell, and taste. What is the other world like? Is the other world a complicated formula of mathematical symbols that could lead us into the higher dimensions where only the privileged few mortals dare venture? In the heyday of slate writing there possibly was, inevitably was, the unknown mathematical formula that would not have been understood then, but could be deciphered with today's technology and scientific advancements. The question that remains is a feeling in my mind of seeing those symbols or whatever they were and of seemingly being so close to a solution, but yet so far away.

I leave my final conclusion, ideas, and assumptions with the reader of this book and those privileged few who would dare venture into the unknown.

Sources

Buckland, Raymond. *The Spirit Book: The Encyclopedia of Clairvoyance, Channeling, and Spirit Communication.* Visible Ink Press, 2006.

Carrington, Hereward. *Modern Psychical Phenomena.* Dodd and Mead Co., 1919.

Doyle, Arthur Conan. *The History of Spiritualism.* Arno Press 1975.

Fodor, Nandor. *Encyclopedia of Psychic Science.* Arthurs Press Ltd., 1933.

Frederick, James M. H., and Olga A. Tildes. *The Silver Cord.* The Christopher Publishing House, 1946.

Jung, C. G. *Psychology and the Occult.* trans. R. F. C. Hull. Princeton University Press, 1977.

Klimo, Jon. *Channeling: Investigations on Receiving Information from Paranormal Sources.* North Atlantic Books, 1998.

Light Of Truth. The Light Of Truth Publishing Company, 1897.

Owen, J. J. *Psychography: Marvelous Manifestations of Psychic Power Given through the Mediumship of Fred P. Evans.* San Francisco: The Hicks-Judd Company, 1897.

Richmond, A. B. *Seybert Commission Report Addendum, 1888.* Boston: Colby & Rich, Publishers, 1889.

Rider, Fremont. *Are the Dead Alive?* New York: B. W. Dodge & Company, 1909.

University of Pennsylvania. *Seybert Commission Preliminary Report.* J.B. Lippincott Company, 1887.

Periodicals:

Lily Dale Chronicles, Joyce LaJudice/Ron Nagy archives.

Morning Star, October 17, 1993.

Psychic Observer, September 10, 1938.

Psychic Observer, September 10, 1943.

To order additional copies of this book,
please send full amount plus $5.00 for
postage and handling for the first book and
$1.00 for each additional book.
Minnesota residents add 7.125 percent sales tax

Send orders to:

Galde Press
PO Box 460
Lakeville, Minnesota 55044-0460

Credit card orders call 1–800–777–3454
Fax (952) 891–6091
Visit our website at *www.galdepress.com*
and download our free catalog,
or write for our catalog.